Understanding Edward

*Inspiring and motivating children
– a guide for parents and teachers*

Justin Collinge

ISBN: 978 1 44664 509 3

Author: Justin Collinge

Published by Pearson Publishing

© 2010 Justin Collinge

Contents

Acknowledgements

Oh to have my children young again so I can do it all again! I am so proud of my identical twins Mark and David and daughter Siân. They have put up with a great deal as I have learned some of the lessons discussed in this book. I dedicate this book to them.

Also to so many others to whom I owe so much:

- My wonderful wife Ali.
- So many dedicated teachers determined to provide the very best education they can under such pressures.
- All you parents who have sought to be all that you can be – again under such pressures.
- The Kaizen Training team, who have brains and hearts the size of planets.

And finally, I dedicate this book to my brilliant parents Joan and Gerald, who believed in me from the start and still celebrate with me every chance they get.

Graham Shaw

Graham drew the cartoons for this book. He is
an international conference presenter and trainer
specialising in advanced communication and learning
skills. He is perhaps best known for his use of fast
cartoon drawings during his training. He also runs
highly popular programmes that teach people how to
use cartoons to make ideas memorable. His one-day
master class 'Cartooning for presenters' has been used
by many major companies in the UK and overseas.
He also has a very successful e-learning version of the
course available on CD-ROM.

To find out more, contact Graham Shaw at:

Web: www.grahamshaw.net

Email: graham@visionlearning.co.uk

Tel: +44 (0)1932 253235

Prelude

Thank you for picking up this book.

When I learned this material it changed me. I learned a bit more about how I came across, not just as a father, but also as a husband and teacher. I also learned how children and young people (and actually everyone else too) make sense of the world and this had an even bigger effect:

> *My important relationships became richer as I understood and valued what was important to my family and friends. (My long-suffering wife says that, for our marriage, it is the most important thing we've ever learned.)*

> *My impact on children changed as I began to put these principles into my interaction with them – both my own children and those I worked with as a teacher. You too will discover how to use the new knowledge to communicate, inspire and motivate more effectively.*

To introduce the idea of what we're talking about I like to use the metaphor of sunglasses. I want you to imagine you have got some orange-tinted glasses, with trendy arms. Put them on right now and look around. Immediately everything takes on that orange tint – well, except orange things which may become a little grey. You can still see everything I can – nothing's hidden, it's just a different shade. After a very short period of time you start to get used to them and soon forget that they are even there. Life carries on exactly the same except you are now seeing it a little differently, and because it is now so normal you forget that other people may be seeing everything with a slightly different emphasis because they have different-coloured lenses.

Now imagine that, after a lifetime of wearing one colour, you were able to take off the glasses and see everything in a new light, literally! And even better than that, you were able to put on someone else's glasses so that now you can see things as they do. That is what this book aims to do. It will show you how to take your glasses off and introduce you to a fresh way of understanding everything around you, giving you an insight into who you are and how you come across that might take your breath away. If that wasn't helpful enough we'll also take that extra step and seek to see what everything would look like if you were wearing someone else's glasses, giving you an insight into what your children see and thus the best way to communicate with them without barriers.

There is so much to get your head around that the book is broken up into phases, giving you a chance to try out the techniques and apply them before taking you further. Phase 1 introduces the first three filters we'll be exploring. This ends with a reflective chapter that encourages you to think through responses and application. You could skip this section but, in my experience, you're much more likely to make good use of the information you're learning if you pause along the way and seek to apply the learning than if you press on to the next step before assimilating the last one. Phase 2 does exactly the same for three new filters. The last two filters explored in Phase 3 have a slightly different feel and are slightly more complex.

One word of warning: if you're looking for a theory book then this isn't it. If you want to learn the background research then there are other books out there that will provide that. This is written to be a practical workbook and is completely focused on the value of learning to improve your relationship with children, be it your own or those you're responsible for. You'll find it easy to apply the information in all the different circumstances of your life, and if it doesn't overflow to affect your relationship with a partner or at work then I'll be surprised and disappointed. However, the aim is to make a significant difference to the way you enjoy that most important and sometimes most challenging of relationships – the relationship with your children.

A quick word about the language used in this book. I use the word 'child' to mean your son, daughter or pupil as opposed to someone around five years old. It would get tedious to always say 'child or young person', so the age range I have in mind as I write is from anyone old enough to talk, up to anyone old enough to leave home.

Every example is based on a real person, though in almost every case the name and environment has been changed for the sake of privacy. In every case gender is not important, unless this is specifically discussed.

It's your choice how you read the book; there's no right or wrong way. My only piece of advice is that you don't just read it, but also seek to do the different exercises. It's so very easy to read a book like this and find it interesting. That is not why it's been written. Once you start to do the exercises and start to notice your filters it will begin to have an impact. It's like the difference between being told about swimming and beginning to paddle and give it a go.

So how about it, fancy a swim?

Chapter 1

Getting started

Some explanation and examples to get you thinking.

We'll call him Edward

Edward was a lively eight-year-old. He was a very sensitive boy and full of mischief and fun. After one of my seminars his mum asked me if I could help. Her struggle with him manifested itself in one very clear (and very common) issue. She was by nature an organised and tidy person. When you visited her house it was always clean, tidy and clear of clutter, except for one room. Yes, you've got there before me. Edward's bedroom was a ... well, actually it was a fairly typical eight-year-old's room. That is to say it was a complete mess! His mum had tried everything from bribery to punishment and nothing really worked. The room stayed messy.

So, could I help? I spent a little while chatting with Edward and noticed something. I told his mum how to rephrase the way she asked Edward to tidy his room.

I'll share exactly what I'd noticed later in this chapter. Let me entice you to turn the page by saying that not only did it work, but his mum gained an insight into the way that Edward thinks, which is quite different from her own way of thinking. Not only was the room not such an issue, but actually something bigger and more important happened; her relationship with her son took an important turn for the better.

And then there is Sarah

Sarah was a lively, enthusiastic and cheerful single mum with a distant and 'difficult' teenage daughter. They went to counselling together but saw little or no change. Things were beginning to get unbearable for them both. I've had teenage children and know how hard it can get, so I offered to share some of what I'd learned. I took Sarah through a short (ten-minute) interview that showed up some of the ways that she processed information. It took maybe another 20 minutes to explain how to work through the same interview with her daughter. I'll share the results of that interview in a little while; suffice to say now that, after Sarah worked through the same material with her daughter, their relationship was never the same again.

And finally we'll just take a glance at Adam

Adam was a long and gangly ten-year-old boy, slightly nervous and with few friends. His mum couldn't cope with him and he lived with his grandparents. I was a class teacher in a middle school and he was one of the 32 children I spent every day with. I was an easy-going teacher with a very friendly style, and I'm ashamed to admit that I didn't like him. He was so needy and poorly behaved and he spoiled the feel of the class with his constant desire for attention. Despite myself, I found myself avoiding him and seeking to distance myself from him.

One thing changed everything. Just one change in my thinking was all it took to change my attitude, which in turn changed everything for Adam. It took all of around 15 seconds to gain my new perspective and, during the following day, Adam's behaviour turned around so remarkably that, at least in school, he never went back to what he had been.

OK, I'm claiming a lot. "15 seconds?" "Never went back?" Like the medicine men of cowboy films selling snake oil, does it sound a little too good to be true? Most of us have a love/hate relationship with simple-sounding answers. We long for easy solutions while at the same time distrusting anything that offers them.

Let me put your mind at ease. What we're about to explore together will feel like taking off that pair of colour-tinted sunglasses and seeing a new reality around you. You will begin to notice things that have always been there, always very obvious and yet, because of our ability to filter the world around us, we've never noticed them before. It's as simple as that. We'll look at some behaviour together and you'll see it in a new light. However, learning to use this information and learning to get out of your habitual way of thinking is more of a challenge. More than ten years on from when I first started seeing things differently, I still find myself learning fresh distinctions and new skills on an almost daily basis.

Since I'm keen to get going and want to be sure you are going to stay with me long enough to learn the wonderful benefits ahead, let me tell you about some of the rewards awaiting you (and by implication some of the cost of missing out).

So what is it that we're going to be exploring together?

It has long been believed that we can only pay attention to a small amount of information at a time. It was suggested that we are potentially aware of millions of different impulses arriving through various means into our neurosystem (Migliore, Novara and Tegolo, 2008). We can become aware of some of these impulses at any time by directing our consciousness towards them. For example, as you read this page pause for a moment and, without moving them at all, become aware of your toes. Can you feel them now? Now, again with no movement whatsoever, become aware of the muscles around your mouth, or the small sounds around you, or your elbows, or exactly how your stomach is feeling, or the temperature of the air against the skin of your cheeks. You haven't created something new, all of these impulses were always there, you've just tuned into them – at the cost of something else you were paying attention to!

The theory goes like this: the very latest research suggests that we can only be consciously aware of three or four things at any one time (Rock, 2009). So to make any sense of this sensory bombardment we've become expert at filtering the world for what we consider important. You're doing it right now. By focusing on these words and giving them your attention you are tuning out of all sorts of other things that you currently consider unimportant. However, a tiny change like the distant cry of a baby, or the squeal of car tyres, or the faintest whiff of smoke and you become alert to a changing situation. You then give something else your attention, making that temporarily more important. This filtering is an essential skill which we can't survive without. Aeons ago, it gave us the ability to notice tiny signals that suggested the presence of a waiting predator. These days it enables us, for example, to stop listening to the noise we're constantly surrounded by (just listen right now and notice how noisy your environment is).

Neuro-linguistic programming (NLP) talks about this need to simplify the amount of information being received to prevent us from becoming overwhelmed. NLP groups the different ways of simplifying as *deletion* (where we completely ignore some information), *distortion* (where we change the information being received into something more reasonable to us) and *generalisation* (where we group things to make them easier to think about, eg we think of 'car' rather than '2003 ice blue Ford Focus Ghia estate with 16-valve engine, part-leather seats and cruise control fitting – when I say fitting it was fitted after manufacture because the buyer changed job and started a lot of motorway driving – he got it from a local garage which offered it for ...'. It's easy to see why we might want to simply think of 'car', isn't it!)

In this book, we'll look at a range of different 'filters' we all use to simplify the world around us. The magic begins to happen as we start to understand how we, as individuals, filter the world. It picks up more power as we begin to notice how our children filter, especially when we can see how their filter patterns are similar to or different from our own. The final step, where the real magic begins, comes when we learn how to adapt our behaviour to suit others' patterns. This is where turbulent relationships can become smooth and supportive and the whole world becomes a nicer place to journey through. Let me give a very personal example. I've been married for 29 years. The day we came across this whole filtering idea and saw how different we were in certain areas, how we saw different things as important, was the day our marriage became better. Almost overnight those areas of recurrent argument smoothed over. Instead of getting irritated, we found ourselves laughing. We began valuing things in each other that we used to complain about. Without question, my wife would say that the day she learned that I processed information through a 'differences' filter pattern was the day our relationship changed.

Instead of getting irritated, we found ourselves laughing

NLP calls these filters 'meta-programmes'. According to Wikipedia, these meta-programmes are *"the more general pervasive habitual patterns commonly used by an individual across a wide range of situations"*. I'm not sure how helpful I find that description, but the key words are 'habitual patterns', ie our ways of behaving that are predictable and consistent. Rather than the slightly clumsy word 'meta-programme', from here on we're going to use the word 'filter' to describe the specific ways we choose to make information important.

That's nearly enough theory for now. My passion is to find things that make a practical difference and so I'm looking forward to getting into the meat of all of this. Before we start, we need to think about one more thing that's really important. What I'm about to say may sound strange but I believe it's a vital part of using this book effectively.

I'm not sure I believe that these filters are totally accurate. Whether they are or not, I certainly do not like anything that seeks to profile people or put them in boxes. My own values say that people are far too complex and wonderful to fit into any box that can be created, no matter how cleverly constructed. Going a step further and putting someone in a box and saying that this is 'who they are' and that this can't change I believe is most unhelpful. Count Alfred Korzybski (an original thinker in these areas) said, *"When you take a word or a label and stick it on a person you create a primitive form of unsanity"*! There are many well-known cognitive style analyses that claim to be able to identify people types in a fairly rigid way. I strongly dislike such claims for two important reasons. Firstly, because they label people as something less wonderful, a little more mundane, completely predictable and locked into certain ways of behaving. I think people are too interesting and too brilliant to be so labelled, and reducing them to fit a category of types or personalities just blinds us to the richness of who they can be. Secondly, and more importantly, whether true or not, I have found such arguments ultimately limiting. It is usually not helpful in the long term to lock anyone into any system and make them unable to escape their particular genetics, upbringing or experiences. As a wise person once said, we are *"fearfully and wonderfully made"*. These filters don't tell us who we are, only how we behave; how we function operationally.

So, if these filters aren't 'true', if they don't give us convenient boxes to put people into, then where's the value? This system is a great model. Like all models it provides a simple way of understanding something complex. It isn't supposed to be true. It enables us to understand and work with people in new ways. Also, while certain traits seem to be consistent, others might be very context-sensitive (eg one thing at school and another at home). I have a very pragmatic way of handling all of this which I encourage you to develop. It consists of two principles:

Principle 1: Since people are complicated and this is just a model I hold it very loosely. I see it a bit like trying to hold a butterfly. Squeeze too tightly and it will die. Hold it too loosely and it flies away. If the model seems to fit then I'll use it and if it doesn't then I'll move on and use something else.

Principle 2: Since people are complicated and this is just a model, I don't fret over what I don't understand. Don't get me wrong, I love exploring the exciting complexity of the human psyche. But for me it's a bit like eating a roast dinner. When I come across a bone I have a choice: I could spend a long time trying to pull it apart and grind it down until it's something I could eat (though by then it's probably become something no-one would want to eat), or I can put it to one side and enjoy the parts of the meal that are digestible. I choose to enjoy the meal rather than feel obliged to pin down every response or comment (to mix my metaphors). This way of thinking is not only more satisfying but it's actually more useful too.

In summary, what we're about to learn is more like a novel than a rule book. Or to use the metaphor from the prelude, we'll take the tinted glasses off and see things that we'd never noticed before. However, don't for a moment believe we're seeing *reality* – we've not reached the bottom, we're just another level deeper, that's all.

Now that's all clear I think we're ready. Let's begin
to explore by looking at Edward, Sarah and Adam
once more.

Edward, with the serially untidy bedroom (ie it felt
like one untidiness simply followed another with no
real space gained by a good tidy up) was driving his
mum mad. Now, before I go any further I ought to
add that my sympathies were with Edward. He was a
lively eight-year-old boy. An untidy room is normal!
However, I was concerned that this was seriously
affecting his relationship with his mum and was just
an example of a big mismatching of expectations and
behaviour – of their *filters*.

I sat down with Edward and asked him a couple of
slightly odd questions. He seemed to enjoy answering
them (as all children I've worked with do). When I
asked him to talk about a couple of pens I'd laid on the
carpet in front of him I noticed a completely different
pattern of answers from those his mum would have
given. Over the years I've got used to spotting these
things and was fairly confident I knew how his mum
would have answered. Because I wanted her to see
how different she was in her filter pattern I decided to
ask her the same question. I used different objects – a
couple of mugs if I remember rightly – and asked the
same questions of her. What was revealed by these
questions was that Edward noticed *differences* between
things while his mum noticed *similarities*. You can
explore the exact questions and answers that these
patterns give and their implications in Chapter 4. The
implication for Edward and his mum was that I told
his mum to use a specific phrasing when she wanted
him to do something. Instead of just telling him what

she wanted him to do, I encouraged her to tell him first that he wasn't going to agree or like what she was going to say.

> *"Please go and tidy your room"* became *"You won't agree with me but I think you should tidy your room before watching TV"*.

Edward's way of processing information was, and I believe still is, to mismatch. He would disagree with most things said to him. (Know anyone like that?) If you were to say to him, *"Isn't it nice weather today"*, he would be most likely to mismatch and tell you about how wet yesterday was. He's not being 'bloody-minded' but this is his way of working out what is being said and how he feels about it. That small change in language meant that his internal response was to mismatch:

> *"Don't tell me I won't agree, I'll tidy my room if I want to!"*

Speaking as a person with a strong Differences pattern I can attest to how effective this is. I fall for it every single time this language pattern is used on me! I recognise it now and won't respond as obviously as Edward did when we used it with him, but actually in my heart I've already reacted. I just sometimes wish my wife didn't know all this stuff!

Before continuing, a quick word about manipulation. I occasionally get criticised as being manipulative and teaching people how to be manipulative. I understand that comment. The line between manipulation and better communication can be a fine one. My personal determination is to build the best relationships I possibly can which includes being the best communicator I can be. One way of avoiding being negatively manipulative is to be completely open about what's going on. I always tell the people I'm working with what I've learned about their filter patterns. Sometimes it's a challenge to make it make sense to young children but they often surprise me with how easy-going and open they are to concepts that adults struggle with a little. We'll talk more about sharing with others in Chapter 16.

One way of avoiding being negatively manipulative is to be completely open about what's going on

Remember Sarah? Communication between Sarah and her teenage daughter had almost completely stopped and hostilities had begun. I took Sarah through a set of questions, all described in the chapters of this book. She learned about herself and went home to ask her daughter the same questions. This is what she wrote to me ten days later:

Dear Justin,

I just wanted to write to thank you for helping me with my daughter Gemma.

When Gemma was constantly upset, miserable and saying that she was 'rubbish', I didn't know how to handle it. I'd never known anyone who was so negative about everything. Her school put me in touch with Child Psychology, but they had an 18-month waiting list and that was too far in the future for me. They suggested a local counselling service as a quicker solution, which it was.

The counselling service was great. We had six meetings to assess how Gemma and I felt about different subjects such as education and home life. We then had a further six meetings to develop action plans and strategies to work together to make things better. The process was a real help but Gemma would still say that I wasn't listening or that I just didn't understand her even though I tried as hard as I could.

By showing me my filter patterns and using the filter interview, you have resolved our biggest problem. We were poles apart on almost every scale. No wonder we couldn't communicate well. We saw almost everything from a totally different perspective.

Now Gemma and I can really talk. We get on better than ever before and have a closer relationship than I had ever imagined. Words can't express how much you've helped us.

I hope you can bring this experience to every parent, teacher and child alike.

What excites me here is that less than 30 minutes with Sarah made such a big difference for both of them. How wonderful! (In fact this letter was an important step in my decision to write this book.)

Remember I talked about a boy in my class called Adam? I wanted to like him but didn't. What happened to change everything? One evening I was complaining about Adam's attention-seeking to a friend of mine and he said something really challenging. The conversation went something like this:

Me: *This boy called Adam is driving me nuts with his constant need for attention.*

Friend: *So give him attention if that's what he needs.*

Me:	*What? I'm not going to let him win!*
Friend:	*Oh sorry, I didn't realise it was a competition.*
Me:	*Um ... er ... it's not ... um ...*

The next day, I gave Adam all the attention I could. I welcomed him to the class in the morning. I asked his opinion. I chose him to help me when I needed it. It went completely against the grain but, guess what, his behaviour changed completely. All I needed was to see it from his point of view and then respond to him from that new viewpoint. Easy? No, actually I'm embarrassed to say I found it quite hard. However I had learned a vital lesson. If I could get out of my own head and into theirs, everything could change. That change in perspective is what this book can help you do.

As you read each chapter you'll see yourself in some of the descriptions; you'll also see your son, daughter or pupil. It won't take long and it will feel quite an easy process. Unfortunately that's as far as some people get. They find the principles informative and helpful and then carry on exactly the same way as they always have done, maybe occasionally smiling when they see one of the filters in action. There is another step to take after learning the principles. We need to see how to apply it and then practise, practise, practise. Some of the moments that have the greatest impact will come from you operating using a different filter pattern from the one natural to you. Imagine learning to write with your left hand (or right hand if you are left-handed). You will probably never be as fluent but you can learn to do it if you are committed. Learning to use different filter patterns is not as hard as changing your writing hand but it does require some focus.

I don't promise an easy road but I do promise three things:

- A sense of amazement as you see things that were in front of you all your life and you never noticed.

- Some real fun as you learn who you are and delight as you discover some of the wonderful complexities in the children around you.

- Better and easier relationships with your children as you learn how to be who they need you to be. To paraphrase Cesar Millan (also known as the Dog Whisperer): it's not about training them, it's about us learning new behaviours that will bring out the best in them.

In the next few chapters we're going to be taking a good hard look at some different filters. You may want to stop during each chapter and ask the questions posed of yourself. That's great if you do. My advice is to get someone else to ask you the questions – it's quite hard to respond cleanly to your own thinking! If on the other hand you want to read on, there are summaries that take you through the filters and help you to identify your own set of filter patterns. In addition, at the end of the book we describe an interview structure that can be used to work through all of the filters in one go.

Most of the chapters describing a filter are divided into similar sections:

- An overview of the filter being considered.

- How can you tell? – This explains how to work out the filter pattern that someone else uses. It includes a question to ask and what to look out for as the child answers.

- Examples – Each filter pattern is illustrated by describing a child with typical behaviour associated with that particular pattern. As you read each description you will recognise some of the children around you. You will also recognise various habitual behaviours of your own. These examples finish with suggestions of how to motivate these people (whilst minimising issues raised by their filter pattern), including helpful language to use.

- Applying this filter – This cites an everyday situation and explores how an individual is likely to respond to the challenges described. Again you will recognise both your own common behaviours and those of the children in your care.

- A summary of how to use this filter in everyday life.

Ready?

Let's start by looking at the three filters that make up Phase 1.

Phase 1

The first set of filters

Direction filter

Frame of reference filter

Relationship filter

Chapter 2

Towards or Away from?

Why do some children do some things straight away and others put things off?

Direction filter

This filter looks at the underlying motivation beneath many of the choices and decisions we make. It focuses on whether we choose something because we want it, or because we don't want to be without it. It shines a light onto whether punishment or reward is important to us.

That's exactly what I want. Now how do I get there?

Towards or Away from?

A Towards child wants to get something and looks forward to a result.

An Away from child will seek to avoid punishment and wants to get away from something.

Our culture tends to value positive attitudes over negative ones and so it is easy to think that Towards might be better or 'more positive' than Away from. However, that is a mistake and it is important to avoid putting our value judgements on these filter patterns. There is nothing intrinsically better about being a Towards person or intrinsically worse about being Away from.

As with all the filters it all depends on context as to whether the specific filter pattern is helpful or unhelpful. (Please note the language – we're still not talking about better or worse.) For example, strongly Away from children have important strengths, but this can be missed if you are strongly Towards and don't value the same things.

Someone using a Towards pattern wants to get something and looks forward to a result. These people tend to be the 'go-getters' and respond well to having the promise of a reward.

Someone using an Away from pattern will seek to avoid punishment and wants to get away from something. These people tend to respond well to having penalties for missed deadlines.

Ultimately, Away from children can grow up to thrive in roles like the emergency services, the medical profession, quality assurance, and any role in which avoiding mistakes is important.

On the other hand, Towards children may become great at finding new markets, sales, motivating others, generating ideas and any role involving taking risks.

Towards or Away from – how can you tell?

Although these filters are all about behaviour, the easiest way to understand which pattern a child is using is by paying close attention to the language they use. Once you learn about these filters you will begin to hear them around you all the time. As you start out getting your head around them, by far the easiest way to learn how your son, daughter or pupil is filtering is to ask set questions. These questions may seem a little strange to the person you're questioning but they are also quite fun to explore. One word of caution: the way they are phrased is often critical, and while you're learning this system, it is better to use the exact words recommended. It is too easy to change the wording a little and inadvertently insert your own filter pattern.

Question

A good question to work out the Towards/Away from preference of a child is to ask:

"What do you look for in a friend?"

If this is a bit personal it works well with various alternatives, such as: *"What do you look for from a lesson?"* or *"from school?"*. If you're a teacher, take care with the school-based alternatives. The answer given might depend on your relationship with the child and they might give you a set of answers they think you want to hear rather than real answers.

Get three answers from them. For example, the conversation could go something like this:

You:	*What do you look for in a friend?*
The child:	*I like someone who likes the same things as me.*
You:	*That makes sense. What else do you look for in a friend?*
The child:	*Honesty.*
You:	*Uh huh, and one more?*
The child:	*Having fun together.*

Encourage them to keep going until you have three answers, but if they dry up then don't worry. If you are unsure later you can always ask them an alternative question and see how that compares to their previous answers. However, it is important to point out that this filter may be context-sensitive – the child may filter one way at school and a different way at home. I tend to assume it's not context-sensitive until I discover it is!

Follow-up question

This is the key question that is going to give you the filter pattern. The previous question simply gave you the information necessary to ask this second question:

"Why is 'someone who likes the same things' important to you?"

It is very important to use exactly the same phrase that the child used. Otherwise your filter pattern may change the results you get. For example, it is not the same to say, *"Why is 'having similar taste' important to you?"*. It may seem the same to you but it isn't the actual phrase that you got originally.

If they get stuck, encourage them to start with the word 'Because'. This will encourage the sort of answer you're looking for rather than some long-winded story they could come out with.

The child will answer in one of two ways. They will either say something like:

> *"Because I like it when we enjoy the same things. Then we can have fun and enjoy being together."*

This is a classic Towards answer, talking about *what they want to get* from friends. Towards people tend to use words like 'want', 'like', 'enjoy', 'love', 'gain' and 'get', and their body language often includes nodding and pointing.

Away from people will talk about *what they don't want* and use words like 'don't want', 'don't like', 'don't enjoy', 'hate', 'scared', 'upset', 'need' and 'avoid', and their body language often includes shaking the head as well as hand gestures that suggest getting rid of something.

A typical Away from answer could be:

> *"Because if you don't enjoy doing the same things then you end up arguing about what to do."*

I know what I don't want – how do I get out of here?

Listen closely to the answer they give. Sometimes people answer by substituting one word for another similar one. For example, when talking about what they look for from a school someone could say, "*I want it to be interesting*". When asked why that was important to them they could answer, "*Because I like variety*". This is a bit of a 'muddy' answer. To me it sounds like they have just exchanged the word 'interesting' for another connected word – 'variety'. At these times I ask, "*And why is variety important to you?*". Then they may go on to say how they hate being bored. Ah ha! This is a classic Away from answer. Some people suggest asking this sort of stacked question, where you question the answer, and then question that answer, and then question THAT answer, until you've done it five times to make sure you've got the real filter pattern. I don't usually work this way for two reasons. Firstly, it's often nice and clear in the first place and digging simply confuses the issue. The second reason I don't like to do this is because you tend to get very irritating!

Once you have an answer, go on and ask about the next criteria they mentioned:

"And why is honesty important to you?"

Listen to the answer and then ask:

"And so why is fun important to you?"

You will find that sometimes you get really clear answers to these questions and it is very obvious what pattern they use to filter. Other times you will get two responses that lean one way and a third response that leans the other way. However, you will generally get some idea of which way they prefer (Towards or Away from). Remember that some filters will be strong in some people and quite weak in others. If this was a spectrum – and I'm convinced it is – then some people will be right out at one end or the other of this filter while others will be somewhere in the middle.

Adrian is a Towards boy

- He likes targets.
- He likes measuring how far he's got on any given path.
- He wants to see milestones on his journey.
- He wants to know when he's succeeding.
- He likes to think about 'the next thing'.
- When planning, he quickly breaks things down into achievable steps.
- He isn't particularly motivated by threats.
- He might miss detail that he doesn't consider important.
- He might not prepare well for future problems (eg exams and tests may not matter that much to him).
- He might take unnecessary risks because he doesn't really grasp the impact of it going wrong.

How to motivate Adrian

Adrian doesn't really feel the impact of consequences so it's not particularly effective to explain what can happen when it goes wrong, when work isn't done on time, when there are minor mistakes, etc. However, he does understand goals and rewards and so it is effective to provide clear steps towards finishing any piece of work and offer incentives if the targets are reached.

You will get the best results by not focusing on issues he sees as 'nit-picking' and letting him express himself freely. Channelling energy rather than controlling it is the key.

Channelling energy rather than controlling it is the key

Allow him to dream and explore new ideas.

Set clear targets and rewards for reaching them. Make it clear how pleased you are when he gets it right and 'dream' with him where possible.

Helpful language for Towards people is:

> "Adrian, if you can get this piece of work finished by the end of today you will be able to start the next piece of work tomorrow. I know that your teacher/the head/your dad [anyone important] will be pleased to see the progress you are making."

> "What are you getting on with right now?" "What's your next step?" "How will you start?" "What are you going to get out of finishing this piece of work?"

Dasha is an Away from girl

- She is motivated by the threat of punishment and/or sanctions.
- Deadlines are particularly helpful.
- She might be quite concerned about detail and good at spotting mistakes.
- She is likely to prepare quite well for tests or exams.
- She tends to take the safer route, avoiding risks where possible.

- She wants to know when she's failing so she can do something about it.
- She doesn't respond particularly to the concept of rewards and dislikes targets (though targets might be motivational if she is scared that she might not hit them!).
- She will tend to be distracted by the need to fix something that is wrong rather than be able to leave it until later.

She wants to know when she's failing so she can do something about it

How to motivate Dasha

Dasha is very aware of consequences and concerned about what will happen if things go wrong or she doesn't understand something or she misses a deadline. Setting Dasha guidelines enables her to steer a course that avoids problems, for example a clearly defined deadline is much more helpful than leaving it open.

When looking at improvement issues it is more helpful to Dasha to look at her common mistakes than to focus on model answers.

Providing clear rules to follow allows her to work within defined limits where she's likely to be happiest. Beware of setting rules that she can't understand or follow – it is likely to discourage rather than motivate her.

Helpful language for Away from people is:

> *"Dasha, if you don't get this piece of work finished today you won't be able to start the next piece of work tomorrow. Then you will keep me waiting for it."*

> *"You don't want to leave this or you'll find you won't be able to do the next bit."*

> *"Where do you think this work isn't as good as you could do?" "What could you do to make it less weak?" "What could you leave out?"*

What if you have both Adrian and Dasha to work with (eg in a group or class)? It might seem easy to look after a single Towards or Away from pattern, but you can often find yourself working with a group where both filter patterns need to be accommodated. How do we actually apply this in everyday life? There's a simple answer for that which we'll get to at the end of the next section on applying this in everyday life.

Applying the Direction filter

The situation

Your daughter is sitting in her bedroom with a piece of work that she should get finished and she's finding it really hard to get motivated. Any excuse to deal with something else takes her attention – an email arrives, the phone rings, someone pops up on Facebook and she decides she needs the loo. She even pops downstairs and offers to help with tea! It's simply not getting done.

The key to being able to help is to know whether your daughter uses a Towards or Away from pattern. If you don't know, or suspect that she's in the middle, then both of the solutions would help.

If she uses a Towards pattern (like Adrian)

Reminding her of the deadline and the consequences of not getting it finished on time will not make a big impression on her. She does know that others are getting on with it and she's going to be late. While she cares about the fact that it's going to be late and will annoy her teacher (again), it simply doesn't give her that urge to finish it off. What can you do to help?

The answer lies in understanding that reward has much more impact than consequence. The cost of not getting it done is not very motivational. The benefits may be. So try to focus on all the rewards of getting it finished. Set her little goals along the way and celebrate in some way when she reaches them. For example, encourage her to chat with her friend only when she's completed a set portion of the work. Or suggest she answers the email only as a prize for getting another part done. Rather than focusing on how unmotivated she feels, which only causes her to feel worse, encourage her to feel great about small steps. In a nutshell, focus on how good it will be to finish rather than how bad she will feel for not finishing it.

If she uses an Away from pattern (like Dasha)

She knows how pleased everyone is going to be when she gets this finished but somehow it just doesn't seem to make any difference for her. One of her friends rings up and reminds her of how much they are looking forward to seeing her once she's finished it. She knows it's important but she just can't seem to focus. Knowing that her teacher will be pleased to see it completed makes little difference. What can you do?

For an Away from pattern, consequence has much more impact than reward. She will be bothered by it going wrong and motivated by avoiding the implications of not getting it finished. So focus on the consequences – make them as important as possible. Help her to imagine the impact of failing to meet the deadline, with her teacher being angry about it, her friends disappointed with her and how it will then eat into her weekend preventing her from going out. It will help her to set small consequences if she doesn't get parts finished; eg if she doesn't get this section finished she won't be able to stop and respond to the email (this may seem the same as saying she can respond to the email once she's finished, but it can have a very different impact). Point out to her how fed up she is feeling and get her to picture herself in two hours time feeling even worse if she hasn't got on with it right away.

As you read through the last few paragraphs you may have found yourself warming to one style and feeling like the other isn't really going to make any difference for anyone. That is your filters talking – pay attention. That preference is giving you an important message about what you find important. It isn't necessarily saying anything about the 'right' or 'better' way of doing something – recognise that people who are different from you will find the other paragraph as helpful as you find yours.

Using such motivational language with groups or classes may appear difficult but it is fairly straightforward and, with a small amount of practice, it can become quite natural. How do you appeal to both types of people? All you need to do is to say it both ways!

> "If you can get this piece of work finished then you're going to feel great, you'll be able to get on with the next thing and you'll be able to get out and enjoy yourself at the weekend, but if you don't finish it off you're going to get all sorts of hassle from [the teacher], the next lot of work won't get started and that might have implications for how much work you're going to have to do for homework."

Can you see how both Towards and Away from are included in that statement?

Summary for using the Direction filter

Towards	Away from
Use rewards	Use consequences
Focus on small, achievable steps	Focus on deadlines
Help them to look at detail	Help them focus on the main task, avoiding being distracted by smaller issues
Provide support for revision, since they may not prepare well	Encourage them to take risks
Value their 'go for it' attitude	Value their care about detail and concern about getting it right
Talk to them about their lack of awareness of consequence and the need to allow for that	

Chapter 3

How do we know anything?

Why your child might not listen to you.

Frame of reference filter

How does a child recognise something as right or wrong? How do they know if it's good or bad?

This filter illuminates the process by which we all make value judgements. It also helps explain why some children follow rules and others don't.

Internal or External frame of reference?

An Internal frame of reference pattern makes judgements based on some *internal scale*. This internal scale may have nothing whatsoever to do with 'reality' (whatever that is). This scale simply provides a way of measuring success and failure, good and bad, right and wrong, necessary and unnecessary, etc. It can be completely divorced from what others think and based solely on some unknown experiences and values.

An External frame of reference pattern makes judgements based on *what other people think*. It is dependent on the opinions of everyone else and measures success and failure by their reactions. It can be completely divorced from what the child feels; in fact sometimes the child's feelings are of such little value that they almost don't exist without responses from someone else.

Internal frame children are good at working in environments where they need to find their own motivation and be self-sufficient. They tend to be good at 'going for it' and can make strong group leaders because of their inner conviction about the way forward. But their strength is also their weakness in that they are not good at listening to advice. They can be difficult to motivate, but when started they are hard to stop!

Teachers often find Internal frame children difficult because they are harder to mould. Internal frame children also tend to be less concerned about following rules and will happily go outside a rule or instruction if they can justify the need to do so to themselves.

External frame children are good at working in collaborative environments. They respond well to correction and will adjust their work accordingly. They are good at following procedures and guidelines, tending to stay within the rules and to meet deadlines. For this reason they tend to be favoured by teachers who find them more malleable, though perhaps less inspirational.

Their weakness is that they need feedback to know whether their work is any good. Therefore they don't tend to work well on their own. They are also poor at self-evaluation, with little idea of whether the work they have done is good enough unless provided with a clear standard to measure it against. Please remember that this goes for anything they have done. They simply don't know if you're pleased unless you tell them in some way. If you are an Internal frame parent with an External frame child, they are going to struggle. You will tend not to say when you're pleased because it's obvious. However, they won't have a clue whether it's good enough or you're pleased with their efforts. You have to learn to be different for their sake.

Internal or External frame – how can you tell?

Like most of these filters, when you become familiar with it you will begin noticing it in the way that people behave and talk. While you're learning to spot it, the best way to know the pattern someone is using is to ask a specific question and listen very carefully to the answer.

This is the question to use when working out the Frame of reference filter:

> *"How do you know when you've done a good job of something?"*

Listen for whether they talk about themselves or others. As is often the case, if they talk about both themselves and others, the first thing they talk about gives a helpful clue. Also watch for whether they point to themselves or use broader sweeping gestures indicating others.

Internal frame of reference

Internal frame of reference patterns are shown by any reference to themselves: *"I just..."*, *"I feel..."*, *"... inside ..."*. Sometimes I've found that strong Internal frame children don't fully understand the question because 'it's so obvious'.

A typical Internal frame answer would be:

> *"I just know it. It makes me feel good. I like it."*

They often point to themselves as they talk, sometimes placing a hand over their heart as they tell you how they feel about it.

Don't bother to tell me what you think, I know just what I like.

External frame of reference

External frame patterns are shown by any reference to other people and their opinions: "*They...*", "*My teacher...*", "*My friends...*". A typical external frame answer would be:

"When my teacher tells me." or "When my friends like it."

Body language often includes hand gestures that indicate someone beyond them, or may point towards an individual if present.

You can also ask this helpful follow-up question:

"And where do you feel that?"

An Internal frame of reference pattern will point to a part of their body (typically their heart or head). An External frame of reference pattern simply will not understand the question!

Rachel has an Internal frame of reference

- She likes working on her own, or in a team if she's in charge.
- She knows very clearly when her work is of a good standard or not.
- She tends to treat instructions as suggestions and won't really understand what the fuss is about when her behaviour is challenged.
- She is quite self-critical and may not take praise particularly well.
- If she doesn't like something she's done there is very little that can be done to change her opinion.
- If she's proud of something she's done then it can be very hard to help her to see how it could be improved – she would rather spend her energy on something more worthwhile.
- She often flouts the rules and is impatient with any rules she sees as unreasonable, especially 'little things' like uniform.
- Teachers may find her difficult and might interpret her confidence as arrogance. Or they may struggle when she doesn't listen to encouragement.
- She can resent having to do work she doesn't agree with or see as valuable.

How to motivate Rachel

Once you understand that Rachel's world is evaluated by a set of invisible rules, things become much clearer. Since she evaluates the world on her terms, it is important to seek to understand those terms. The only way to motivate a person with a strong Internal frame of reference is to use their own standards. Simply telling them that in your opinion something can be improved, or that her behaviour doesn't measure up to some set of standards, doesn't help much. Rachel is equally hard to encourage – telling her that a piece of work is exceptional makes little difference unless she can see it for herself.

The only way to motivate is to seek to guide her as she makes her own decisions and evaluations.

Helpful language for Internal frame people is:

> *"Rachel, what do you think of this piece of work?" "If you were to improve it, what could you do?" What is best about it?" "What is weakest?" "How could you make that part stronger?"*

> *"Why do you think this rule was made?" "How would it affect you if everyone else broke this rule?"*

Mark has an External frame of reference

- He needs to have feedback and is a little lost without it.
- He finds it hard to stay motivated if he doesn't have a clear set of guidelines to follow.
- He tends to take suggestions as instructions.
- He works well in a collaborative environment.
- He can be a good follower or leader as long as there is clear feedback and lines of communication.
- He tends to follow the rules, but beware – the 'rules' could be ones made by his peers.
- He may respond well to positive correction, enjoying being able to please the teacher.

- He may find working alone difficult because he swiftly becomes unsure whether his work is of value or not.

He tends to take suggestions as instructions

How to motivate Mark

Once you realise that Mark makes judgements about everything based on feedback, he becomes quite easy to motivate. Providing regular information about how he's doing and where he could improve is all he really needs. Reward systems work quite well and feedback from other people can be especially helpful. Since he won't be able to judge whether a piece of work is good enough, he can get demotivated by working on his own for too long.

Mark won't respond particularly well to being asked his opinion and it may be important to teach him techniques for assessessing his own work. The best way to do this is to provide a clear scheme to measure his work against.

Lacking any clear internal feeling of what's expected, he may copy peers' behaviour, either good or bad.

Helpful language for External frame people is:

Anything that refers to his work and gives him a clear idea of what you feel about it.

Remember that he will take suggestions as instructions, so be careful about saying off-the-cuff ideas that you haven't thought through!

Applying the Frame of reference filter

The situation

Your son has completed a piece of work and is going to hand it in tomorrow.

How he feels about it and its quality may well depend on his Frame of reference filter.

Internal frame of reference (like Rachel)

If he has an Internal frame of reference pattern, he may feel one of two ways: either satisfied that it's of the standard required and happy to hand it in, or uncomfortable about the quality and really uneasy about handing it in but not sure what else to do. The important fact to be clear about is to understand that, although he holds his opinion in high regard, it's not necessarily accurate! He may love what he's done, he may hate it. What is important to him is how he feels about it rather than some external required standard. This means that it may be great and everyone loves it, but unless he feels the same way he is in danger of dismissing their views. Or it may be poor and everyone tries to tell him this (gently of course), but again he dismisses their views because his opinion is more important to him than theirs.

If he has a strong Internal frame of reference, then this is the question to ask him: "*What do you think you could change to make this even better?*". This appeals to his own frame of reference rather than imposing a different one that he doesn't see as relevant. You can go on to ask about other people's opinions as long as you phrase it to be within his frame of reference: "*What do you think others would say you could change to make it better?"*. If you're going to try this then it really helps to agree together in advance that he will pay attention to whatever you say.

The ideal is to encourage him to remember that his judgement is not necessarily the only valid one and to determine to respond to others' comments whether he agrees with them or not.

External frame of reference (like Mark)

If he has an External frame of reference pattern, then the problem is that he doesn't have a strong feeling about the work. He isn't sure whether he likes it or not, whether it's good enough or not. He always likes to pass it by someone else first and get their response before finally handing it in. That's fine. That's good practice. However, it may help to protect him from lots of different points of view which would back him into a corner, trying to please everyone and ending up with a middle-of-the-road piece that pleases no-one. The best answer for him is to ask only a few people (maybe two – eg you and a friend) whose opinion he trusts and use them as his sounding board. He needs to make the decision to trust their viewpoint and go with that. He also needs to be disciplined about not passing it around to anyone else. One or two positive responses from people whom he knows will be honest are more than enough.

Summary for using the Frame of reference filter

Internal frame of reference	External frame of reference
Always refer to their internal judgements (eg *"What do you think would be a better response?"*)	Always refer to what others think (eg *"Wouldn't your friends prefer this sort of response?"*)
Give ideas on how not to appear arrogant	Give plenty of positive feedback about anything and everything
Look at how rules/guidelines/laws have a positive impact on their life (rather than why they should be obeyed). Remember that this is hard for an Internal frame person to understand!	Understand that they may respond to suggestions as instructions
Understand that they process instructions as suggestions	Peer pressure and needing peer support may be a very important feature
May work better given space to make their own mistakes	May not work well alone
Value their ability to know themselves and what they like	Value how sensitive they are to others' feelings rather than getting frustrated by them not having the same opinions

Chapter 4

Is this the same or different?

Why some children get bored quickly; and how to deal with someone who always seems to disagree with you.

Relationship filter

Look at two similar objects. What do you notice? Do you notice what is the same about the objects or what is different? Which do you notice first?

Like most of the filters, it can be quite surprising to realise just how consistent people are in the way that they notice things. And like most filters, if a person is strongly orientated towards one extreme or another it is likely to have a huge impact on all they do and say. This is because it will affect everything they notice, and that in turn affects how they relate to the world around them.

Similarities or Differences?

Similarities children notice *links*. They see how people, objects and events relate to each other. They perceive their environment as an interconnected web of cause and effect. They tend to be good at understanding systems and people. They like routine and enjoy being comfortable and knowing what's expected.

Differences children notice *changes*. They see small differences. They perceive their environment as a collection of distinctions. They tend to enjoy change and will alter a routine just to see what happens – even if the new way of doing something is not as good as the original way. They can be terrible at following procedures. Differences people can be seen as argumentative because their way of processing information is to mismatch. To a Similarities person, that mismatching comes across as either negative or arrogant because they can hear it as someone having something better to say.

Similarities or Differences – how can you tell?

If you ask the suggested questions for finding out the filter patterns from the last two chapters, you should get reasonably clear answers. This filter can be a bit more subtle.

An easy way to get a child talking about their filter pattern is to ask them to talk about similar objects. It helps if the objects are things from their own world – for example, a couple of toys or pencils – but avoid using anything they are likely to have an emotional link to such as a favourite toy. I often lay two pens side by side and say:

"Tell me about these two pens."

(That phrase is carefully worded; if using this technique, I advise you to keep to this wording.) I choose these pens very carefully. They are very alike (eg both biros) rather than completely different (eg a felt pen and a biro). I also put them facing roughly the same direction. I've also used glasses, books and cruet.

(Tip: You could just use the picture below – show it to them and ask, "Tell me about these two pens".)

A typical Similarities answer would be:

"They are both pens. You write with them. They both have ink. They are sitting on this table, pointing the same way. They're about the same length. They both have clips. What do you want me to say?"

A typical Differences answer to the same question would be:

"That pen has writing on it. One is probably black ink and the other I don't know. I like this one. They are pointing in slightly different directions. That one is longer than the other. What do you want me to say?"

Notice that the Similarities pattern thinks of them as the same length (because they are near enough) and a Differences pattern thinks of them as different lengths. The Similarities pattern notices that they are facing the same way (again, they are near enough) and the Differences pattern notices the ... well, difference. To me, with a strong Differences pattern, I struggle to understand how anyone could say that these pens are the same length or facing the same way. A strong Similarities pattern is likely to see the previous comment as petty and nit-picking.

Jenny notices similarities

- She likes routine.
- She likes to know what's going to happen next and isn't particularly fond of surprises.
- She can get disturbed when plans change unexpectedly.
- She can get anxious when uncertain about the future – either immediate or distant.

- She enjoys seeing links between things and learns best by making links between something new and what she already knows.
- She is quite good at seeing how people and things relate to each other.
- She responds well to timetables and likes agendas.
- If she follows instructions she will follow them faithfully.
- She finds comfort in the safety of a known pattern.

How to motivate Jenny

Because Jenny sees similarities, she responds well to having links shown to her. If she's not doing well, it will help her to understand if you tell her about another time when the same issues occurred.

Jenny likes routine and so if her work becomes of poorer quality it might be worth checking whether there has been a change to some routine that's important to her. Although there can be moments when she fights against boredom and rebels against the pattern, in the end she will always 'come home' to a safe routine.

She will learn from making links, so it helps her if links are made as plain as possible. For example, referring back to earlier situations, going back over what's happened beforehand to see how we got here, or comparing this situation to other ones from the past all reinforce the picture Jenny is building up in her head.

Helpful language for Similarities people is:

> *"Jenny, this issue is the same sort of thing we faced before when we were doing [something else]." (Even if they feel very different to you, it is amazing how Similarities people will find those links anyway.)*

> *"In what ways do you think this is similar to what we learned before?"*

> *"When have you felt this way before?" "What is the same about this situation compared to that one?"*

Jon notices differences

- He sees all the little differences between things, even when they are almost imperceptible to others.
- He notices when things don't match.
- He enjoys change.
- He fights routine, preferring to find his own way rather than follow another. If he has to 'do as he is told' he might change something in small ways.
- He is poor at following instructions, choosing to make it up.
- He likes surprises.
- He would rather alter something 'to see what would happen', even if that change is for the worse.
- He mismatches all the time. This can be seen as disruptive because he appears to be constantly disagreeing.
- He is poor at spotting links and so can be out of his depth when expected to see how his behaviour or performance can affect others.
- He might be poor at following timetables and agendas.

- He gets bored and fidgety quite quickly and will respond well to being given something new to do.

How to motivate Jon

The secret to motivating Jon is to understand that he will mismatch whatever is said. Therefore reverse psychology can be quite powerful. Telling him that he will disagree with what you're about to say is an excellent way of getting him to agree with you!

Boredom is quite a big motivation for Jon. He might work poorly simply because he needs variety rather than predictability. He can react to feeling constrained by routines. However, because he can be very sensitive to small differences it can be relatively easy to change his routine. Even very small changes in everyday tasks may be enough to keep him on track. (Even apparently petty changes can be enough – eg using a different colour pen. Insignificant to many, such a change can be enough to keep Jon performing well.)

Helpful language for Differences people is:

"I don't know whether you are going to agree with me, but ..."

"You're not going to like this, but I think you need to finish this piece of work."

"You remember how we fixed that problem? The same thing isn't going to work here. This is going to need something new."

Applying the Relationship filter

The situation

You go shopping with your daughter every Saturday morning. It used to be a nice family moment but has gradually turned into an increasingly difficult time. Now you seem to have an argument about it every weekend. Why can't she just enjoy what she's always enjoyed?

Similarities pattern (like Jenny)

Over the years, you've probably got used to the way that your daughter responds to, and builds, traditions out of the things that you do as a family. In fact you may have noticed that she really doesn't like change and, as you look back, you realise that most of the difficult times with her happened when she was facing big changes – changing school, moving house, etc.

This means that you may have got very comfortable with the idea that she wants routine and likes doing what you've always done in the way you've always done it. If this is the case for you, then the challenges that come with puberty may catch you off-guard. Although she wants, and even needs, routine, she is also in a phase of her life when independence from you and doing things in the same way as her friends suddenly become more important. Where she gets her sense of belonging and similarity might shift from you to her friends and it may be much harder for you to see the links.

Part of the answer is to focus on the emotions rather than the behaviour, ie making sure you build on any opportunity to make her feel safe in her relationship with you, rather than worrying too much about any specific activity.

Take comfort in the fact that she will be happy to be seen in public with you again in a few years' time!

If your child has a strong Differences or Similarities pattern, or if you do, then this is an enormously important filter to be aware of. It can have an impact on everything they (or you) do. It can change the way they think about everything. So where there is a conflict in this filter's patterns, it will usually cause conflict in relationships.

Differences pattern (like Jon)

As your daughter grows up and gains her own sense of identity, she will increasingly need to change things around. The cosy family routines you have enjoyed up to now will fragment as she discovers her 'power' to ring the changes. If this is happening then make sure you choose your battles carefully – some things are not worth a fractured relationship. However, if you decide that shopping together is something worth fighting for then make it easier for her by changing anything you can and see whether each change makes it better or worse. Go to a different shopping centre, go at a different time, go by bus instead of by car. Be prepared to let go of the coffee shop you have always stopped in and try somewhere different each week.

If you pay close attention to how she reacts to each change, you will be able to craft an experience that is a rewarding one for both of you.

Summary for using the Relationship filter

Similarities	Differences
Like routine so, if upset, look to see if routines have been changed or uncertainty has been increased	Like change, so create small changes in routine and encourage them to make small changes
Make plenty of links between what they are learning now and what's gone before	Allow them to make their own choices where possible
Create timetables, agendas and mini-traditions	Plan in some surprises where possible (eg a surprise sandwich filling in their packed lunch)
Value their consistency rather than getting frustrated by what you could consider unimaginative or boring!	Value their different way of looking at things rather than getting frustrated by it!

Chapter 5

Working out the Phase 1 filters

This chapter helps you to work out who you are, who they are, and begin to see how these things work together.

Here, we'll pause and explore a little more to give you a little more insight into your own set of filter patterns. The better you know yourself, the better you will be able to respond to the particular needs of children. If they have similar filter patterns to you then you will know how to make the most of that. If they have different patterns then this may well give you insight into what you can do differently to suit what they need from you.

Direction filter

Think of a goal you'd like to achieve and write it down. It doesn't need to be very detailed, just a phrase or a word to represent it is enough. It does help to write it down rather than just hold it in your mind.

Now ask yourself *why* that goal is important to you. Write down the first three things that come to mind, starting each one with the word 'Because'.

Do it now, before you read on.

As you look at your three answers, can you see a pattern in terms of Towards or Away from? Did you write reasons that were about what you want or what you want to avoid?

Here's how I answered this:

> My goal was a financial target to hit by the end of the year – I simply wrote down the amount.
>
> My three reasons for wanting that goal?
>
> Because I don't want to miss the specific advantages that this goal represents for me.
>
> Because I'd like to earn a little more than I currently earn.
>
> Because I want to avoid a sense of failure if I don't hit it.

In this example, the first and last reasons have a clear Away from pattern. The middle one sounds more Towards. If you have a similar mixture, it can mean a few things:

- You might be a mixture and not strongly one pattern or the other in the context you chose. However, even with a mixed answer you can usually see a leaning towards one side of the spectrum or the other.
- You might need to think of some more reasons.
- You might have a different pattern hiding behind your phrases. I regularly ask a follow-up question to dig down a little deeper. For example, my middle answer sounds Towards in direction. But what if I ask myself why I'd like to earn a little more? The answer is a clear Away from – *"Because I don't like not having enough money to be able do what I want to do"*. It can really help you to ask these sorts of follow-up questions. As explained in Chapter

2, I've heard some people recommend you keep asking until you've gone down five levels. (So my next question could be, "*Why is 'not having enough money to be able to do what I want to do' important to me?*".) When the answer seems fairly clear I tend to trust the first answer and remember how irritating it can get to keep digging!

Please remember that this is 'not true'! It's not about who you are so much as how you behave. It's also quite context-sensitive and so may be true about one particular area but not about another. It's a helpful pointer, that's all. Also, please remember that there is no intrinsic benefit to one pattern over another. Both are important and both can provide vital skills. One is not better than the other. However, most people tend to feel that their pattern is, underneath all the positive and politically correct language, better in some way than the other pattern. I think that's quite a healthy feeling as long as you also acknowledge it to be completely wrong!

Having done this exercise, have you got a feeling for who you are when it comes to the Towards and Away from filter? If not, then try a different goal and do it again or get someone to ask you the questions outlined in the Direction filter chapter (Chapter 2).

Frame of reference filter

This tends to be a little easier to work out than the Direction filter. Like all of these filters it works better if you get someone else to ask you the question, but you can try it yourself, in which case ask the question of yourself out loud and answer it out loud. If you can't do that because of people around you, then it's better to write down your answer than to simply sit and think about it.

Ready? Here's the question. Remember to either answer it aloud or write it down:

"How do you know when you've done a good job?"

For those of you reading on and not doing the exercise I recommend that you stop, put the book down and do it properly. You'll gain much more from it than simply reading on.

Have you done it? Promise?

OK, so what was the first answer you gave? Many people give lots of answers and it's quite interesting to note the first thing that came out of your mouth (or flowed from your pen). There are two possible ways of answering: you can either talk about what other people think or you can talk about how you feel. Which did you say or write first? An answer that refers to what others think shows an External frame of reference and one that refers to what you think or feel shows an Internal frame of reference. It might be worth looking back at Chapter 3 to see what each style means in terms of strengths and weaknesses.

Once you've done that, let's look at who you are when it comes to the Relationship filter.

Relationship filter

To determine where you come regarding the Relationship filter, write down a list comparing this year to last year. It doesn't matter whether you want to think about this in terms of home life or work. Try to write five things or more.

Done? You should now have a list of things comparing this year to last year.

As you now go back through the list, notice whether you have written about things that were similar or things that were different. Did you comment on things that have stayed the same (eg *"I'm living in the same house"*) or things that changed (eg *"I've painted the walls a different colour"*)? Did you comment on working in the same office or that you had a new team member? Or did you comment on a mixture of the two? If it was a mixture of similarities and differences, which did you talk about first? What comes to mind first is often a good indicator of what's important to you.

There are four options here – did you notice similarities, or differences, or similarities first and then differences (around 65% of adults have this pattern), or differences first and then similarities (around 20% have this pattern)?

Now you have some idea of whether your pattern is similarities- or differences-orientated, it might be worth looking back at Chapter 4 to see where your strengths and weaknesses might lie.

Summary for using the Phase 1 filters

Below are some suggestions for responding to everyday situations that may arise using the Phase 1 filters.

The situation: The child won't do something, eg tidy their room or do their homework	
Towards	Set simple rewards and targets Example 1: *"Just think how good you'll feel once you've got it done – and tell you what, when it's finished I'll let you choose [something that they don't normally get to choose]."* Example 2: *"Get this bit finished and then stop and pick up the next bit after a break."*
Away from	Make the consequences of not completing it very clear Example: *"Just think how bad you're going to feel if you still haven't finished this and so then you aren't able to [do something they will want to]."*

Internal frame of reference	Appeal to their sense of what's best
	Example 1: *"Which bit of this task will have the biggest impact on you once it's finished?"*
	Example 2: *"If you were to expect this from someone else, what reasons would you give to encourage them to finish it?"*
External frame of reference	Refer to how others will feel
	Example 1: *"Just imagine how pleased your [teacher/mum/sister] is going to be when they see this all done."*
	Example 2: *"Give me a call when it's done because I'd love to look at it and tell you how well you've done."*
Similarities	Link it to other things that have happened
	Example 1: *"Remember how good you felt last time when you got this done."*
	Example 2: *"What happens at school when people don't do their homework? Would you want that to happen to you?"*

Differences	Remember to use the reverse psychology technique
	Example 1: *"You're not going to like this but I think you should get it finished before tea."*
	Example 2: *"Everyone will expect you to be late with this."*

Of course everyone is a mixture of all of these patterns so here are some examples of how you can combine these ideas.

Towards^(t), Internal^(int) & Differences^(diff)	*"You're not going to like this idea(diff) but what about setting yourself(int) some small steps to help get it done(t) – what steps(t) would someone like you(int) choose(diff)?"*
Away from^(af), External^(ext) & Similarities^(sim)	*"Remember(sim) the trouble(af) you got into last time(sim) when they told you(ext) how poorly(af) you'd done?"*

Phase 2

The second set of filters

VAK (or Modality) filter

Inside/Outside filter

Chunk size filter

Chapter 6

Filtering information through our preferred senses

As you read this chapter and **see** (visual) how to apply it, you're going to like the **sound** (auditory) of how it may help you **get to grips** (kinaesthetic) with all sorts of current problems.

VAK (Visual, Auditory, Kinaesthetic) filter

A few words of introduction are needed before we get too far into this filter. There are several different frameworks that seek to split people into certain styles that suit their learning. However, recent research into learning styles has not supported the idea that people fit into these tidy categories. Furthermore, most evidence suggests that limiting people to one preferred learning style is actually counter-productive and the pupil performs worse than if given a mixture of styles. (The exception to this is when dealing with very low achievers or those with learning difficulties, where there is some evidence that finding a favourite style of learning and sticking to it may help.) This fits perfectly with my experience as a teacher where I found, the more varied the learning environment, the better it seemed to suit everyone.

So contrary to what some teach, I do not suggest that an insight into this filter gives an insight into how to focus the learning patterns of a pupil.

Having said all of that, I have found insight into this filter has given me an amazingly powerful tool for responding in the moment and providing what an individual needs. So when a child is stuck, either with homework or when having difficulty explaining what they are feeling or thinking, this filter can help you know what to look for and how to respond appropriately. Rather than a rule to stick to, this is simply an extra tool you can use when needed.

The theory goes that everyone has a preferred way of remembering sensory information. Most of us will reference memories through *visual* stimuli (what we saw), *auditory* stimuli (what we heard and said) or *kinaesthetic* stimuli (what we felt or did). There is a fourth common representational system called *auditory digital* which includes a mixture of the others.

The most efficient way of storing information is to do so visually. However, non-visual children will tend to use non-visual cues to remember visual information. For example, they may remember the feel (or perhaps smell) of an old jumper they once wore before they can remember what it looked like.

The real key to success is twofold. It is very helpful to discover how your child or pupil is filtering information and be able to respond appropriately to that. But you must also be able to discern your own natural tendencies since you will automatically favour your own strengths, which are not necessarily the strengths of those you want to communicate with. That's fine for children with the same strengths as you but can be quite limiting for those who are different.

VAK – how can you tell?

All the other filters work by asking questions and listening closely to the answers. This one's different. This time you need to *watch* closely. We give away how we're thinking by the way we move our eyes. This might sound strange at first but as you watch for results it will become very obvious. The first time I came across this I was very sceptical. Then I asked some people some questions and was amazed by the responses I saw – people really are consistent in where they look when they access information.

However, let me stress that rigorous testing is yet to prove this theory. Maybe it's just an interesting phenomenon which is yet to be understood. Maybe people are so incredibly complicated that this is a simplification too far. My way of handling this is the same as it is for all the filters. It's just a model, it's not 'true' – so if it seems to be helpful, work with it until it seems not to be – and then do something else! Remember holding that butterfly?

Asking any question that makes a child remember a past event will work, though it's worth being careful to avoid questions that have very strong emotions linked to them, like when they got into trouble or finally achieved a goal. For example:

"Tell me about last Christmas."

Or *"Tell me about your last holiday."*

Or *"Tell me about last weekend."*

If you don't see clear eye movement and they simply stay looking at you then the answer is too available to them and they didn't have to 'go inside' and think about it. The solution to this is to make the question harder – eg *"Tell me about last Christmas Eve"* or *"Tell me about the second day of your last holiday"*.

As the child accesses their memories, they tend to look in a certain direction.

Looking upwards, or going out of focus into the distance, suggests that they are remembering information primarily through a visual cue – ie they make a *picture* in their minds (*Visual*).

Looking sideways suggests that they are remembering information primarily through *sounds (Auditory)*.

Looking downwards suggests that they are remembering information primarily through *feelings and/or actions (Kinaesthetic)*.

See the diagram below for help with this. For the moment, don't worry too much about whether they look off to the left or to the right. The left/ right direction and some of the more complex eye movements you might encounter are explored in Chapter 12.

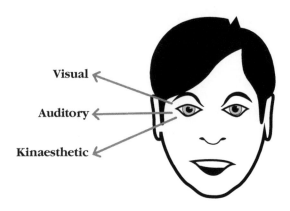

Visual

Auditory

Kinaesthetic

As well as the eye patterns, there are various other things to look at and consider. The way someone is sitting, dressed, how they talk, even the shoes they're wearing all give further clues as to their Modality (VAK) preferences.

Visual	Kinaesthetic
Dress smart	Dress comfortably
Look smart – eg combed hair, well-ironed clothes, care about how they look including making sure they wear matching colours	Can look a bit scruffy – eg hair not well brushed, shirt untucked, don't really care about how they look including wearing colours that don't really work together
Sit up straight	Slouch as they sit
Talk faster and higher with few pauses	Talk slower and deeper, with pauses marked by noises like 'err'

Visual	Kinaesthetic
Footwear often gives it away – but be careful to look at how they are maintained rather than their design (shoe design often reflects the modality of the parent who chose them – how they are kept reflects the modality of the child). Shoes of visual children tend to look smart and freshly polished	More likely to wear shoes that are well worn-in and look 'comfortable'. They'll wear trainers if the situation allows it

Before you write to me telling me that the kinaesthetic column is describing any typical teenager, let me encourage you to look at the teenager in context – ie with their peers. It becomes very obvious when you have a group to compare an individual with. Although they may all be dressed casually, when you look closely it becomes clear who cares about how they look and who doesn't. I was teaching a group of GCSE students some revision skills recently and, as they walked in, I could see some clearly visual and some clearly kinaesthetic individuals by comparing them with the norm within the class. The unironed shirt or the carefully tied tie, the clean or scruffy shoes, the brushed or tousled hair were all clues that were obvious when able to compare them to others like them. This was soon backed up by seeing how they sat – straighter than average or more slouched than average.

Auditory people can be a mix of both of these, but give themselves away the moment they speak. They will enunciate every word quite clearly to make sure it's heard correctly. They talk a bit like they are a radio announcer telling everyone what is going on. (A good friend of mine who is very Auditory visited my home a little while back and, when the phone rang, announced clearly to everyone, *"that will be the phone"*. Of course it was the phone, it was my phone! His way of processing the information was to announce it.)

Auditory digital people can show any of these signs. They tend to talk about things 'making sense' and prefer things that are ordered. The key trait is the power of their internal dialogue. Please note, everyone has an internal dialogue, it's just that Auditory digital people listen to it more closely. So ask them what they're saying to themselves right now and watch how easily they answer the question.

Andy is a Visual thinker

- He tends to dress well and cares about the way he looks – eg he will care if his hair is messy or if his clothes are dirty.
- He sits up fairly straight in his chair.
- He talks reasonably fast and at a high pitch.
- He breathes from high up in his chest.

- He uses language based around how things look:

  "I see that"

  "I like the look of them"

  "Picture this ..."

  "Focus on ..."

  "It appears that ..."

  "Imagine that ..."

- Colours are important to him.
- He might show some skills at drawing or painting or photography. He will be good at seeing subtleties that may escape others, eg small colour changes.

How to motivate Andy

It will really help you to know which pattern you prefer. If you are the same as the child you want to motivate, then there is no problem. It's when you are different that it becomes important. Remember, we all like people who are like us. So the more you can appear like Andy, the easier it is for him to respond positively to you.

For each of the patterns, part of the secret to motivation lies in using their metaphors, pictures and language rather than your own. You can literally 'speak their language', ie use the very same words and phrases that they do. For Andy, it will be phrases like:

*"Let's **look** at this more **closely**."*

*"Use your **imagination** to **picture** it as though it were finished – what does it **look** like?"*

Andy is likely to be quite affected by how his surroundings look. An untidy environment can be a constant distraction. While clashing colours may bother him, bright pictures and posters may inspire. According to research by Pat Wyman, any information put above eye level (ie above your eyes when you are sitting down) is twice as likely to be remembered than information you look down at to access (Wyman, 2001). So putting inspiring quotes or current information that Andy needs to be aware of above his eye level will be significantly helpful for him. (Please note this is true for everyone, not just visual people!)

Information put above eye level is twice as likely to be remembered

Vicki is an Auditory thinker

- She tends to sit with her head to one side.
- She can appear not to be listening because she doesn't necessarily look at you when you're talking to her.
- She is sensitive to noise and might be quite bothered by things that others don't notice – eg the hum of a fan.
- She is quite distracted by others talking or by the TV.
- She may like music and sometimes uses it to cover up other distracting noises.
- She tends to talk loudly and clearly.
- The words that you use and she uses can be of great importance to her.

- She uses language based around how things sound:

  "I like the sound of that."

  "Listen, I've got something important to say."

  "That rings a bell."

  "I hear you ..."

  "I'm all ears."

  "... tune in/tune out ..."

How to motivate Vicki

Like Andy, Vicki will respond more positively to suggestions posed using her preferred language.

*"I have to **say** that I like the way you've **listened** to me, and I know that what I've **said rings a bell** with you. It **sounds** to me like you're doing all the right things and I look forward to **hearing** you **tell** me about it next time we're together."*

Vicki is unlikely to make progress in an issue without the chance to talk it through or at least to write about it (she'll say the words in her head as she writes). Be aware of her needs for noise or silence. Some auditory people find comfort in bustle around them; some need it quiet to be able to think.

Jack is a Kinaesthetic thinker

- He doesn't worry too much about how he looks. He might appear scruffy because he is more concerned about comfort than appearance.
- He tends to sit comfortably and may appear to be slouching.
- He talks slowly, with a deeper tone and uses 'thinking noises' – *"um..."*, *"urr..."*, *"hmm..."*.
- Like his speech, his movements are deliberate.

- He breathes from lower in his chest.
- He may be good at practical things, good with his hands and may like sports.
- He is quite affectionate and isn't shy about responding physically.
- He uses language based around how things feel:

  "I like the feel of that."

  "I can't get a grip on that."

  "It slips through my fingers."

  "... make contact ..."

  "... tap into ..."

  "...in touch..."

How to motivate Jack

Reflect back the language that Jack uses, preferably in the same tone and pitch.

*"Now you've got **hold of this**, just think how you'll **feel** having **done** the right thing."*

Be aware that how he's feeling about something is going to be more important than how it looks. For example, if he's feeling demotivated then encouraging him to tidy his room is unlikely to make him feel different, whereas giving him a more comfortable chair is. Sitting down and having a one-to-one chat is much less likely to do him any good than getting out for a brisk walk to talk it through.

Auditory digital

There is a fourth pattern some people use. This is where a person keeps a running commentary inside their head. It's a bit like an Auditory pattern, but instead of needing it to be actual sound, they are telling themselves what to think all the time.

Juan is an Auditory digital thinker

Auditory digital thinkers can be a mixture of Visual, Auditory and Kinaesthetic and so may appear to be one or another at different times. The thing to remember is that there is a conversation going on inside their head that no-one else has access to.

- He tends to be quiet in school. He doesn't tend to process his thoughts externally because he's talking to himself inside.

- He might come back to you later on, after the class has finished, sharing his thoughts.

- He likes logical steps and is happiest when he breaks things into clear sections or patterns.

- He may have a really great internal dialogue – constantly encouraging himself and pushing himself on. Or he may be constantly undermining himself – telling himself that he's not good enough or reminding himself of how badly he did last time. Because this all happens internally, it is not easy to tell that it's going on. However, if he has a poor internal dialogue, he will be 'beating himself up' every chance that he gets.

- Because of the internal conversation, it is not always easy to tell how he has got to a certain point. Sometimes he's talked it all through at length – just not with you!

How to motivate Juan

Always remember that whatever he says, he's already discussed it internally. This means that it's not easy to get 'clean' answers and sometimes it's worth taking the extra effort to discern how he's feeling behind the answers he initially gives.

Helpful language for an Auditory digital thinker is:

> "logical", "process", "know", "makes sense", "decide" - plus a mixture of all the other language from the other VAK filters.

> "Juan, it makes sense to think about the next step you need to take with this work."

Applying the VAK filter

Your VAK preference allows you to do all sorts of things well, while stopping you from being good at others. The secret is doing what you do well while finding a way of getting someone else to do the things you do badly!

The situation

Keith is working on a project and not feeling inspired. He looks at the messy desk around him, full of bits of paper with various ideas scribbled on them. He knows he needs to get the work done before the end of the week and is not sure what to do.

Visual thinker (like Andy)

Keith is inspired by what he sees (either by what is actually in front of his eyes or by how he is picturing it internally). If he's stuck, change what he's looking at!

First, get him to tidy up the environment. Give him a visually pleasing environment to work in.

Second, give him some colour. Perhaps change the colour pen he's writing with, or the colour paper he's writing on. What if he were to change the screen from black text on a white screen to something a bit more interesting – eg white text on a dark blue screen? How does that feel? Or yellow on a black screen? Is that any better or does it distract him? Maybe he needs to try something more subtle like changing the white background to a pale yellow. How does that feel?

Third, encourage him to create a mind map (spider diagram, concept map, tree diagram, etc) showing clearly where he's got to so far, and then begin to split the rest of the work into different 'branches' using colours, text and pictures to show what needs to be done.

Fourth, STOP! Ask him to close his eyes for a moment and picture the whole project completed. What does it look like? Can he see it all finished? Ask him to imagine his teacher praising him as he gives in the completed project. Fix that in his mind's eye. Now ask him to visualise the steps that need to be completed to get him to that place.

Fifth, if he's still not feeling like getting on, then change his point of view in a very literal sense – get him to sit somewhere different for a while. Maybe even just changing place around the desk will make a difference. Maybe going and working in a different place entirely, eg the library, might help restart his imagination.

Auditory thinker (like Vicki)

He is more inspired by how something sounds to him (perhaps by what he is actually listening to or maybe by that internal soundtrack running inside). So if he's stuck, change the track he's listening to!

First, find someone to talk to. If he is on his own, encourage him to learn to tell his goldfish or dog about where he's got to and why he is currently stuck. Sometimes all it takes is to verbalise it and he will discover the answers for himself.

Second, if he hasn't got the answer from the first step, then invite him to tell someone (such as yourself) what the issue is and then repeat it back to him. Encourage him to notice the answers welling up inside as he engages in dialogue with you.

Third, get him to find a way of audibly recording the way forward rather than having to write it – PCs and Macs are very good at voice-to-text recognition these days.

Fourth, change the background noises. Ask him to be very alert to the effect the different changes have on his concentration. For example, he might like certain types of music but find they distract him when playing in the background. It may be that he needs to find somewhere else to sit for a while where the noises are more complementary to his thought processes. Sometimes the rewards outweigh the distraction. For example, if he finds he can sit and work for twice as long if there's music on than if he is in silence, it may be worth the distraction that the music is causing. Perhaps soft music stops him from listening to the TV in the other room. There is anecdotal evidence that instrumental music is less distracting than that with vocals.

Kinaesthetic thinker (like Jack)

He is inspired by how he feels and what he does.
So if he's feeling stuck, then change what he's doing
and how he's feeling. (Have you noticed that this isn't
rocket science? Most of these filters are actually very
obvious when you stop and think about them. This is
the beauty of it. All this book is seeking to do is to help
you do just that – stop and think about them!)

First, he can change how he feels by changing his
physiology (how he's holding his body), so move!
Any movement he makes will help him feel differently
about things. Maybe take a walk to think things
through before continuing, or just have a good stretch.
Could he go and work somewhere else for a while?

Second, we can also change how we feel by changing
our focus. Ask him to notice how he has been thinking
about this project and to list as many ways as he can of
continuing from here with a different feel – eg he could
write the next section from a different perspective (it
might need editing later), or he could imagine he is
five years in the future looking back and describing
the project to someone. What if he were to ascribe
different positive emotions to the different sections of
the project and seek to feel that way when working
on each section? (For example, the beginning section
could feel exciting, the middle section confident, and
the end reflective.)

Third, doing something will help him make a fresh
start. He could take those bits of paper scattered
around the desk and start creating groups or
connections between them. Perhaps he could make
a mind map out of the pieces of paper. Move them
around his desk into different arrangements until he

hits one that feels best. He could change other things, like writing instead of typing (or vice versa). He could change computer or pen.

Fourth, if he's still stuck, get him to do something different. It's usually unproductive to carry on just trying harder, hoping to find some inspiration. Find some way of continuing the work in a different mode. For example, he could swap from dealing with details to looking at the overall picture (or vice versa).

Summary for using the VAK filter

The situation: The child is upset about something		
Visual	**Auditory**	**Kinaesthetic**
I can see you're upset. What is it that you imagine might happen? Can you picture it happening in a better way?	I can hear you're upset. What do you think I'm going to say about this? Tell me what sounds like a good way forward to you.	This is obviously quite a rough situation for you. Can you tell me exactly how you feel and what would help you feel better?

Chapter 7

Inside or Outside thinker?

Do your children process information quietly inside or more noisily outside?; and why encouraging them to talk to their dog may be a good thing.

Inside/Outside filter

Most children have a clear preference for how they like to think about things. They may like to do so by internally processing it, pondering the alternatives, spending time alone, and working it out until they know what they think and they're ready to share. Others need to think externally – they almost need to see or hear it outside of their own brain before they know what they think. Everyone tends to want to do both; the interesting part to notice is what they want or need to do *first*.

Hmm – just give me a while. I need some time to reflect on this.

Inside thinkers tend to '*go inside*' and think about things before they are ready to talk about them. They will need some space and can get tetchy if asked to give an opinion about something before they've had that inner time. If challenged, they need time to reflect on what they've done before they are in a position to talk about it sensibly. You can often see Inside thinkers lose focus as they go inside. They stop looking at you and look away, their faces going flat as they stop responding. They can be frustrating for some because they don't react fast enough.

Outside thinkers need to *think 'externally'*. They often don't know what they think until they've said it and have had the chance to hear what it sounds like. They can get frustrated if required to think about something rather than talk about it. If asked to 'sit there and think about the issues at hand', they actually can't! They will often just fidget.

They often don't know what they think until they've said it

Inside thinkers find Outside thinkers frustrating because they talk before thinking it through, they don't give enough time to processing an issue and often seem to make decisions without enough thought. Outside thinkers find Insider thinkers difficult because they won't communicate – they seem unwilling to just talk about things.

Inside or Outside thinker – how can you tell?

If you stop and think about the child you have in mind then you can probably already tell which filter pattern they use – whether they need to process their thinking inside or outside.

If you're not sure, then a good question to ask is:

> *"When you've got an important decision to make, do you prefer to think about it first or do you talk it through with someone straight away?"*

The thing to listen out for is which they want to do first.

Inside thinker

An Inside thinker will want to have space before they are ready to talk about it. Therefore a typical Inside thinker answer is:

> *"Well, I like to stop and think things through a little before I'm ready to discuss it with others."*

Often you will know the answer well before the actual words come out of their mouths because they will need to stop and process the question inside before they answer. Usually Inside pattern people will pause to consider the question (ie process it inside!) before giving an answer.

Outside thinker

An Outside thinker will want to have someone to talk to from the beginning. They will put off thinking about it until they get that opportunity.

A typical Outside thinker answer is:

> *"I find that chatting things through with others helps me to work out what I'm thinking about it myself."*

Again, watch closely and you may notice that they explore the question with you rather than pause to consider it – that is Outside thinking happening in front of your eyes!

Supporting questions

Occasionally children find it hard to think of what they do. It may help to ask them to talk about something they have already decided and work through how they made that decision. Helpful pointers can be heard in the answer to questions like the following ones (in these examples a positive answer suggests an Outside pattern):

> *"Do you find it helps to talk about issues you're facing?"*

> *"Do you sometimes find yourself answering your own question when chatting?"*

> *"Do you sometimes talk to yourself?"*

> *"Do you ever start a sentence with phases like, 'I'm not entirely sure what I'm saying here but...' ?"*

Alison is an Inside thinker

- She needs to be given space to think about things.
- She doesn't know how she feels about something until she's given time to think.
- Asking her to give an opinion without giving her the space to think can be quite frustrating for her.

- If in trouble, she needs some time before she's ready to take on board any consequences.
- Her teachers (and parents) can find her frustrating because she won't simply say what's wrong.

How to motivate Alison

When she is struggling, Alison will benefit from being given a bit of time. She needs to work through her internal feelings or dialogue before she's ready to deal with any decisions or consequences. It could be easy to interpret her quietness as non-cooperation. However, that quiet moment is her cooperating as best she can.

Jason is an Outside thinker

- He has a need to talk about everything.
- He doesn't know what he is thinking until it has been discussed with someone – anyone!
- He isn't very good at thinking things through on his own, and finds talking to himself helpful.
- He's discovered that asking questions out loud often releases answers for him without needing an answer from the person he's talking to.
- His teachers (or parents) can find him frustrating because he talks 'all the time', often merely saying what he's thinking.
- He might start conversations with statements like, *"I'm not quite sure where I'm going with this yet ..."*, or, *"I don't really know what I want but ..."*.

Just being able to talk about this has helped so much.

How to motivate Jason

When he's struggling, it will not help Jason to give him time to think about things. He needs someone to talk to and doesn't have a helpful internal dialogue.

He may appear to want advice but is actually often just looking for a chance to 'externally process', so won't understand if you get hurt when he doesn't take your advice, or even listen to it! The best thing to do is to understand and simply be that sounding board.

Applying the Inside/Outside filter

The situation

Carina has got into trouble at school. You aren't clear about the circumstances but suspect you need to take some action to make sure she's learned her lesson.

Inside thinker (like Alison)

The classic mistake with an Inside thinker is to ask them to talk about things before they are ready. To insist they 'just say what they're thinking' is really unhelpful. The best thing you can do is give them a little time to think about it. Maybe give them a time period where they know when you're going to ask them for more details but be ready to give them longer if they need it. This is the time when sending them to their room to think about what they have done is the right thing to do.

Carina's strength is her ability to work through something and come out with answers. Her weakness is that she isn't very good at involving others in that process (the truth is that, at some level, she doesn't really need them).

It may be worth explaining to Carina how she processes so she can begin to offer what other people need. For example, where she has to work in teams it will help her to have some phrases to use which will help the rest of the team feel involved in the process instead of Carina working everything out on her own and only sharing once she's finished.

Outside thinker (like Jason)

The classic mistake with an Outside thinker is to give them space to think about the implications of what they've done. Just because you may need this does not mean that everyone functions the same way. If an Outside thinker, time on her own will simply frustrate Carina until she tunes out of the whole thing and starts doing something completely different.

The answer is to find ways of helping Carina to externalise her thought processes in safe environments. Being able to talk in a non-judgemental environment is very important. It is well worth learning how to do that – to just be there and listen without making her feel judged. After all, she is simply working out what she is thinking – what you're listening to is not a finished thought. If you simply cannot emotionally provide that safe environment then it may be worth thinking of a place where she can talk freely – perhaps to a coach or teacher or grandparent. Having a safe person to talk to, who will just be there and allow her to externally think, is a really valuable asset to cultivate (I don't know where I'd be without mine!).

It will also help Carina to learn how to think externally without needing to talk to someone – creating charts, mind maps, etc can be a good way of doing this. Finally, it is worth talking to Carina and being explicit about how she works, and explaining in advance that you understand that there will be times when she sounds like she's asking for your opinion while all she's really doing is finding out what hers is!

Summary for using the Inside/Outside filter

Inside thinkers	Outside thinkers
Need time to go inside before they are aware of how they feel	Need some way of expressing themselves (talking, writing, drawing) before they know how they feel
Need to be given space to think before they can tell you about anything beyond basic facts	There's no point asking them to sit still and think about 'what they've just done'
Are more self-sufficient	Are more dependent
Are less confident in group situations	Tend to be confident in groups and come across as affable

Chapter 8

Do they want the detail or the overview first?

Why being petty may be helpful; and why your child may completely miss the point.

Chunk size filter

Does your child want details or an overview first? People seem to naturally tend towards either detail or the full picture. They either like to get involved in something straight away, or like to stand back a bit and see the bigger picture before they are comfortable about getting involved. Some people are good at doing both; some people are only good at one or the other. Many pupils fail because either they got so engrossed in the details (eg agonising over grammar and punctuation) that they missed the really important things (eg getting an assignment finished on time). While other pupils fail because they didn't concern themselves with the specifics (eg reading the question properly) because they were so focused on the final outcome (eg the importance of this exam).

A Detail (or Small chunk) child may be excellent at dealing with facts and figures, where small differences could be the deciding factor between success and failure. They may tend to immerse themselves in something and can become so fixated on getting it 'just right' that it becomes impossible to finish. Sometimes they can be very skilled at seeing the next step and problem solving. They are happiest when dealing with the actual bits and pieces that make up a process, whether that's physical items or data. They can get lost and demotivated when asked to 'chunk up', ie to think about the bigger picture. They tend not to be good at setting goals but prefer to get on and work within someone else's timeframe or success criteria.

An Overview (or Big chunk) child may be excellent at seeing what needs to be done at a broader level. They quickly get bored by lots of information and want to know the 'big picture'. They can often be dreamers who generate all sorts of possibilities. This can often be seen from a very young age. They are happiest when not bogged down by the need to get each step right – 'good enough' is their mantra. They can quickly get demotivated by having to deal with what they would see as petty issues. They will often be leaders within their peer group but may lead confidently down a disastrous road because they haven't paid enough attention to the smaller needs of the journey. As they say, *'the devil is in the detail'*.

Small chunk or Big chunk – how can you tell?

A good question to use to work out which Chunk size pattern your child uses is:

> *"If you were about to start a new project at school, would you want to know the details [timescale, how many words, working on your own or with others, etc] or the overview [what it's for, how it fits into the rest of the work, etc] first?"*

(You may need to make it clear that they can have all this information – the question is about which they would like to have *first*.)

With young people, you could ask:

> *"When you want to decide whether to read a book, do you try to get a feel for the whole thing first or do you dive in to read a small section to see what it's like?"*

It should be quite obvious whether someone likes the detail or the overview. The key here is which they would go to first.

A typical Small chunk answer is:

> *"I'd want to know how you want me to work on this and just how much I need to do."*

A typical Big chunk answer is:

> *"I'd want to know what's it's all about and understand what you're after."*

It's all about whether the objectives and vision take the person's attention or whether they quickly get involved in details and process issues.

What amazing details on the ends of your antennae!

Tim is a Small chunk person

- He is happiest when dealing with details.
- He tends to be good at spotting small mistakes.
- He may be good at troubleshooting and creating ideas for the 'next step forward'.
- He is not good at seeing longer-term issues that may arise.
- He gets frustrated with people who seem to talk in vague terms and don't supply the relevant details to keep something 'grounded'.

How to motivate Tim

Make sure he has plenty of information and let him sort out his own way of handling the information. Tim probably likes those moments where something fails and needs solving. He is likely to enjoy dreaming up a possible solution, trying it out and then creating new solutions until the issue is resolved.

Helpful language for Small chunk people is:

Use 'solid' words and talk in 'grounded' concepts. Tim doesn't particularly like metaphors, principles or other such abstract ways of thinking.

Louise is a Big chunk person

- She loves to explore concepts and ideas.
- She is good at abstraction.
- She can be quite visionary in her way of looking at a process and seeing possibilities.
- She quickly gets frustrated by people who insist on talking about the details and exactly how it's going to work.

- She often misses small errors, partly because she doesn't see them as very important and partly because she doesn't stop long enough to notice them.
- She's not very good at troubleshooting unless it involves overall direction and outcomes.

How to motivate Louise

Allow her to dream. Give her the space to explore outrageous ideas. She almost certainly isn't really suggesting that they would all be good ideas so much as exploring them to find something that would be good. Ask her opinion about the bigger issues and release her where possible from everyday repetitive tasks. Give her roles that provide the opportunity to play with different ways of succeeding.

Helpful language for Big chunk people is:

> Louise likes concepts. She may use metaphor to try to express the wider issues in her brain. She will tend to work in abstractions rather than concrete ideas.

Applying the Chunk size filter

The situation

Nadja has been set a new project – it's an important piece of work and counts towards a final mark.

Small chunk size (like Tim)

Nadja grabs hold of the project and gets stuck in. She loves the detail and enjoys working out the first steps to take. She's good at seeing the next step and is happy sorting out what's needed for each step. Her strength is in caring about the fine details. Her weakness is that these details can overwhelm her and cause her to miss the whole point. There are many times when getting the main point through is good enough, and worrying about how tidy a diagram is or feeling the need to explain everything is not helpful and is wasting time that could be spent on something more valuable. For example, 80% of the marks in many exam questions can be gained in a few short remarks and, if time is tight, it's much more profitable to move on than to try to cover all bases to get the last 20%.

Big chunk size (like Louise)

Nadja steps back and takes a look at the whole scene, deciding on priorities and timescales. Maybe she will make a mind map or even a project planner. She may sketch out subtitles and possible content for each section.

Her strength is in being able to see the whole wood as well as the trees and remembering what's important. Her weakness can be that she gets bored by the detail and so doesn't follow through with her big picture plans, instead being distracted by the next big picture project.

Summary for using the Chunk size filter

Small chunk	Big chunk
Appeal to their need for, and enjoyment of, detail	Appeal to their desire to avoid nit-picking and share the broad vistas with them
Value every time they take care of the small issues – whether placing cutlery just right, taking interest in how things work or 'fussing' over something you think is unimportant	Value every time they notice bigger issues, whether in family politics or in simple observations in life
Help them not to miss the bigger issues. You have two important roles:	Help them not to miss the important details. You have two important roles:
• Keep an eye out for those bigger issues and point them out	• Keep an eye out for when detail is important and help them deal with it properly
• Teach them how to do this for themselves	• Teach them how to do this for themselves

Chapter 9

Working out the Phase 2 filters

Who you are, who they are, and how these things work together.

VAK filter

One of the easiest ways of getting an idea of someone's Visual, Auditory or Kinaesthetic preference is to get someone to look at their eyes while you ask the questions listed in Chapter 6. If you want to know your own preference (it's helpful to see how you think compared to your children), then get someone else to ask you the questions while watching your eyes. Remember that this is an interesting hint and suggests your preference. There are several other things you can notice to support, or challenge, this 'diagnosis'.

At the end of Chapter 6 there is a table outlining the dress code, sitting position, pace of speech and even shoe preference of different patterns. Have a look through those and decide where you fit.

Remember we are all a mixture of all of these. We don't fit nicely into any box, no matter how well it's crafted.

Inside/Outside filter

Think about how you (or your child) tackles a new project. Do you spend time chatting with your friends about it first (Outside)? Or do you spend time thinking through the issues before you're ready to talk to others about it (Inside)?

Do you tend to go quiet when you need to think about something (Inside)? Or do you tend to get noisier when you need to think something through (Outside)?

Do you find it fairly easy to work out your opinion about something entirely inside your own head, even to the point of considering different options before choosing what you think is the best one (Inside)? Or do you find it almost impossible to think something through internally, and talk to yourself if there isn't anyone else to talk to about it (Outside)?

Chunk size filter

Do you (or your child) find details annoying and people who obsess about them petty (Big chunk)? Or do you find talking about big issues a distraction from being able to get on with the task at hand (Small chunk)?

When tackling a project of some sort (eg planning what to do at the weekend) do you focus first on the bigger issues such as main choices, how people will feel, outcomes (Big chunk)? Or do you tend to think first about the small detail such as deciding what to wear (Small chunk)?

Where does your attention naturally go – to the outcomes and the big picture, or the details and the next step?

Summary for using the Phase 2 filters

Below are some suggestions for responding to everyday situations that may arise using the Phase 2 filters.

The situation: The child won't do something, eg tidy their room or do their homework	
Visual	Create something visual to summarise the end result, eg a pie chart, a 'thermometer' recording where they have got to, or stickers Say things using their vocabulary, eg *"Just imagine how this is going to look when it's finished. Can you see how important it is? Picture yourself holding the finished item."*
Auditory	Talk it through with them. Get them to describe what they're going to do first Put some suitable music on to accompany the work. Make sure they get the chance to tell someone else when it's finished
Kinaesthetic	Focus on how great they will feel once it's finished Use their language to motivate, eg *"Imagine yourself curled up on the couch watching TV, enjoying the fact that everyone's pleased with you, and relaxing knowing it's all done."*

Inside	Give them plenty of space to think about the consequences of both doing it and not doing it. Allow them some time on their own to plan how they're going to get it done
	They may prefer to do it on their own rather than with your help
Outside	Ask them to talk about what they think needs to be done. Get them to give you five reasons why this is worth doing
	They may prefer to do it with your help rather than on their own
Small chunk	Focus on the details of what needs to be done rather than giving lots of reasons for it to be done
	Break the task up into small steps and celebrate as each step is completed
Big chunk	Focus on the reasons for completing the task; don't get involved too much in what needs to be done

Here are some suggestions of what to say to appeal to different mixtures.

Visual[v], Inside[i] and Small chunk[s]	*"Spend a little time imagining[i and v] how many things will be different[s] when it's finished.* *Can you plan out[i] a flow chart[v] which we can fill in as we complete each step[s]."*
Auditory[a], Outside[o] and Big chunk[b]	*"Come here and tell me[a] what you think[o] are the main reasons[b] why you need to get this finished."*

Phase 3

The third set of filters

Options/Procedures filter

Time perception filter

Chapter 10

Options or Procedures thinker?

Why your child ignores your carefully created lists of what to do next; and why they keep telling you a story, when all you wanted was a 'yes' or 'no'.

Options/Procedures filter

Does your child think in straight lines? This filter, more than some of the others, is about the way children (and of course adults too) think things through. Some children like to look at all the options available and make a choice based on some criteria that they consider important. Other children will be confused by lots of choice and would much prefer to work through an issue sequentially.

An Options child loves to create *possibilities* and find *new ways* of doing something. They can be a little overwhelming in the way that they tackle something since they will come up with more and more different ways of achieving the same objective. (This is especially true when combined with a Differences pattern.) They tend not to be very good at finishing things off since they may perceive that to finish something will limit their options. However, if they believe that by completing something they will then be offered a wide range of different opportunities, they will tend to get frustrated by the need to complete it and may even finish poorly.

A Procedures child likes *process* and *structure*. They are most comfortable having a bulleted list or, even better, a numbered list to follow. They like to see a clear start and end to something they need to do and can get frustrated when an agreed process is not followed. They tend to be more interested in how to get something done and not too worried about why it's being done. Procedures people tend to be good at starting and finishing things. They like to know where it starts, make the start, work through the steps required and then finish. They tend to be good at following rules because they value those rules. They tend not to be so good at thinking flexibly about a problem.

Options or Procedures – how can you tell?

Ask any question that starts with the word 'why' and enquires about a choice they have already made. For example:

> *"Why did you choose to watch that on TV?"*
> *"Why do you like wearing those clothes?"*
> *"Why do you like [a friend]?"*

The key issue in the question is that they need to perceive that they had some choice and it isn't something forced on them by a parent or teacher.

After asking the question, you are listening for whether they talk about criteria behind their choice or tell a story.

Typical Options answers are:

"I'm watching this because I like to watch a bit of TV after school, I enjoy this sort of thing and I've got 30 minutes before tea."

"I'm wearing this because it's my favourite colour, my friend has got one like it and there was nothing else clean for me to wear."

These answers give a set of *criteria* by which to measure the choice that they made.

Typical Procedures answers are:

"I'm watching this because I came home from school and I like to relax a bit before tea, so I turned the telly on to see what was on. Then I remembered that this was on. I saw it last week and enjoyed it."

"I didn't really choose to wear this. When I got up this morning and opened my cupboard, it was there alongside the other clothes that mum bought me for my last birthday. So I put it on and here I am."

Procedures children tend to see life as a sequential *story* and so when asked 'Why?' will answer with a story rather than criteria. They will substitute the word 'Why?' for 'How come?'. If asked about 'choice', they will tend to see events as part of a continuous storyline and, therefore, reasonably inevitable with little choice being made.

Loads of ideas. No idea where to start!

Fatima is an Options child

- She likes choice.
- She is good at creating possibilities and seeing options where others get stuck.
- She is happiest when allowed to explore her own way of doing something.
- She does not follow the rules very well, seeing them as guidelines for those with less imagination.
- She gets excited when planning to do something new, but is poor at seeing things through to the end.
- She is often quite good at juggling several things, keeping them all going at the same time.
- She gets frustrated by people who see only one way of doing something or who work sequentially through a list.
- Procedures people will find her difficult because she never sticks to the point and sees it through.
- She may dress slightly unusually, trying out new mixes of clothes.

How to motivate Fatima

Fatima works best with space to explore rather than feeling pinned down to a fixed way of doing things. Her creative spark is one of her true talents and, if this is smothered, she will tend to lose any passion for what she's doing. If she's struggling, then the best thing to offer her is the opportunity to find as many ways as possible to make things better for her. She'll respond much better to that than being given a set of possibilities.

Because she will not be very good at completing a project, it is worth recognising this and supporting her at these times.

Helpful language for Options people is:

> Use words and phrases that create possibility such as: "opportunity", "unlimited", "infinite", "chance", "release", "break the rules", "what else", "option".

Jeff is a Procedures child

- He likes to start at the beginning and see it through to the end.
- He will get frustrated if regularly prevented from finishing things off.
- He likes to know where he is in a process and will always be able to tell you the next step.
- He may like plans and bullet points and anything that represents where he is in a sequence.
- He finds it hard to tune into more abstract issues like how he's doing generally, and will answer such questions by relating them back to concrete steps.

- He finds Options people difficult because he will be looking for a clear answer and not the various choices that are being offered.
- Options people may brand him 'dull' or 'lacking in inspiration'.
- He will work hard to see something completed and doesn't mind if the task is reasonably repetitive.

How to motivate Jeff

Jeff thrives in an environment where he knows what has to be done next. If he's finding something hard, it's probably because he is unclear about the process or because he is in a changing environment where what he was going to do next has been changed. To get the best out of Jeff, give him plenty of structure and try to keep things working in predictable ways – like homework time and 'family traditions'. Let him know what he's achieved so far and ask him what he's going to do next.

Helpful language for Procedures people is:

> Use words that create certainty and a sense of sequence such as: "first", "then", "last", "next", "process", "the right way", "trusted", "what next", "finish", "start".

Applying the Options/Procedures filter

The situation

Your child is not listening to any advice and constantly breaks your rules (eg chores, language, bedtime, getting up).

Options thinker (like Fatima)

Give plenty of choice rather than expect them to do it
your way. The secret of success here is to give choice
about things that don't matter, as this hides the fact that
you are giving no choice about things that do matter to
you. For example, you can give a choice like this:

*"I don't mind whether you want to do it right now or in half
an hour."*

You have given them a choice about timing while
passing by the fact that they have no choice about
actually doing it!

So, with the example of bedtime, find ways of offering
choices that don't affect the thing that's important
to you. For example, if the time is the issue then let
them choose whether they read or watch TV or use
the computer before settling. If attitude at bedtime is
the issue then you could ask them to think of as many
ways as possible for getting to bed and try each one
out on successive days (eg brush teeth after tea to save
time later, put pyjamas on under clothes so they can
change really quickly, or experiment with sleeping at
the other end of the bed). Try anything that focuses
their attention on possibilities rather than the issue of
going to bed.

Be aware that their strength is in looking at things
and seeing possibilities. They are at their best in fast-
moving environments, constantly coming up with new
ideas to meet the changing conditions. Their weakness
is shown up in any situation when obedience is
paramount, when safety is of particular importance
or when getting something done in a set way is more
important than flair. You may need to be flexible with
them and adapt to the fact that they constantly change

the rules to suit their newest idea. While they may love change, be aware of the fact that their friends, teachers and parents may suffer from change fatigue!

Procedures thinker (like Jeff)

Their strength is found within a process. By creating a clear pathway with measurable milestones along the way you can create momentum for them and help them towards your end goal. Where they are out of their depth is when things are more flexible and the goalposts move regularly. Because they tend to like to stick to the rules, they assume everyone else will too, and can be completely blindsided by sudden change.

The secret of success for a Procedures child is to offer set ways of doing things with measurable steps along the way. For example, if bedtime was the issue then work with them to create a series of steps that gets them to bed at exactly the right moment. Maybe devise a way together of being able to tick off each step. For example, it could look like this:

- 8.11   Brush teeth
- 8.14   Put on pyjamas
- 8.18   Spend time with mum or dad (alternate whose turn it is)
- 8.35   Read
- 8.50   Turn the light off

NB It is vastly more helpful to design something like this together so they feel an ownership of it rather than having it imposed on them by you.

Summary for using the Options/Procedures filter

Options	Procedures
Like to have plenty of choice	Like to understand where on a list of steps they are
Like to vary how things are done	Like to follow a sequence, eg will enjoy recipes, or a set of instructions
Are good at spotting opportunities	
Are poor at seeing things through	Are poor at handling things when they don't follow a plan. Tend not to like sudden changes
To get compliance, offer choice about things that don't really matter to you	To get compliance, get them to turn an action into a set of measurable steps

Chapter 11

Out of time or In time?

Are you worried about your child sitting out and not taking part? Don't be!

Time perception filter

Does your child throw themselves into things or do they prefer to stand back and watch? In my experience this filter makes more sense with regard to older children (of ten and older) than younger children.

Most people can imagine time as something linear, with the past stretching out in one direction and the future stretching out in another, usually opposite, direction. Children particularly are happy imagining this sort of thing and tend to be happy 'playing along' with this imagery rather than struggling with 'reality'. This filter asks about where they see themselves in relation to that line. It gives a helpful insight into how children handle themselves in various situations.

Out of time or In time – how can you tell?

The following instructions take you through discovering a child's pattern in this filter. It may be helpful to try taking yourself (or get someone else to take you through) these instructions so you are aware of your own pattern. For this filter we need to get a bit more involved than in the previous filters.

First, ask the child to imagine they could point to their past. I know that's a strange question but don't let them get too hung up about it because the answer they give isn't too important at the moment. If they simply can't imagine pointing in a direction to suggest their past, then encourage them to pretend that they can do it and so do it anyway.

Many point behind them, though don't be surprised when they do something different. I've known people point straight up or down. One said their past was a ball hanging in the air in front of them.

Now ask them to do it again but this time point to the future.

Many people will point straight ahead of them – that's especially common for those who pointed at their past as going off behind them. Again, don't act surprised if they give an unexpected response – just roll with it.

You should now have two lines representing their past and their future. Next you need to do something that some people find easy and some more difficult. Ask the child to take that past line and, if it's not there already, drag it around to their left so they can see it off to their left-hand side. If it was behind them then maybe it's easiest for them to imagine simply turning sideways on so that they can look down it. Alternatively they could imagine pulling it around into view. If possible the best place for them to put it is somewhere going off at an angle in front of them. Then we need to do the same to their future line. Ask them to drag that one so that they can see it clearly, again preferably off to an angle in front of them. See the diagram overleaf for the ideal place to put these lines.

Future   **Past**

It doesn't really matter which side the child's past or future lines are, they just need to be able to see them both. However, it is important that the child is not sitting or standing on either line; sitting next to them is the best place.

Now let's make them a little more real by putting some events onto them. Ask the child, as they look down their past, to put some events onto the line – their last birthday, their earliest memory, last Christmas, etc. Tell them to put four or five things on it to make it a little more real. Then do the same with the future line. Where would tomorrow's breakfast-time go? What about their next birthday – can they imagine the point on this line where their next birthday might go? Ask them to look far down and notice where their twentieth birthday would go.

We're nearly there now. Here's the question we've been building up to for the last few minutes: does the line they can see go in front of them or through them?

Or to put it another way, the present, the right now moment, is that inside their body or are they looking at it?

A strange exercise finishing in a strange question. Let's now have a look at what their answer shows.

The line was in front of them

This suggests that they perceive time to be something just slightly *removed* from their direct experience. It's almost like they're sitting back and observing life go on. This is an Out of time pattern (neuro-linguistic programming, the discipline that created this model, calls this 'Through time', which many people find a bit confusing so I'll stick with 'Out of time'.)

The line was running through them

This suggests that they perceive time to be something that happens right here and now and they're *in the middle of it*. We call this In time. Instead of the slight removal that an Out of time person feels, In time people experience the highs and the lows of life. It may mean that they enjoy life more when things are going well but suffer more when it's not.

Kath is Out of time

- In class she tends to sit back and let the others get involved.
- She tends to keep her opinion to herself and may help pull things together at the end of a discussion or argument.
- She's quite good at seeing the whole wood as well as the trees.
- She stays cool in an emergency, reacting appropriately rather than in a panic.
- She finds it hard to 'switch off' – she is always aware and rarely completely relaxed and just having fun.

- Some people might say of her that she's a little 'cold', which is quite unfair – she cares deeply about people but just isn't as gushy as some.
- At a party she's much happier sitting back and watching than being in the middle of the action.
- Her strength is that she keeps her cool; her weakness is that she isn't sure how to get hot!

Atul is In time

- In class, he gets involved and argues with the best of them, though he may lose the point of it all in the immediacy of the discussion.
- He can be a bit quick to react and doesn't always think about the consequences.
- He is known at school for being fun, though when he's low he does tend to spread that around too.
- He finds it easy to switch off and is skilled at immersing himself into whatever environment catches his attention.
- At a party he's happier throwing himself in than sitting back and watching.
- His strength is his enthusiasm for the task at hand; his weakness is a lack of awareness for what might happen next.

Exam tomorrow? I can't think about that now!

Using the Time perception filter

This is a bit different from the other filters in that whatever their normal pattern is (In time or Out of time) it can be helpful to learn to be comfortable using the other pattern. It simply takes practice. I've taught this to many people and had some great feedback about the results it's brought. Like the process to find out their pattern, it may sound a bit strange, but if you give it a go I suspect they'll enjoy it.

First find a bit of room to stand in. They will need space in front and behind them. Now get them to draw their time lines again. They may need to imagine themselves back where they were at the beginning and drag themselves around, or they may find they've already developed the flexibility to put their past and future lines in front straight away. It's helpful to put a few dates on the lines like before to make them a little more real.

Part one: Make sure they can see the past and future lines connected into a single line clearly – either going through or in front of them – and then take a step. If they saw the line in front of them, then ask them to take a step forwards into the line (it's important to take a step with them so that you go with them to the new place they experience). Ask them how different it feels to experience time right now. Once they're comfortable in that place, ask them to step back out of time (and you go with them), so they can see the line in front of them again and notice the different feelings that they feel when looking at the moment rather than experiencing it. (I did warn you that this was a little strange. Just go for it and see how it feels.) If, on the other hand, they were already in the line, they need to take a step back and spend a while acclimatising themselves to how it feels to look on, slightly removed from what's happening right now. Once comfortable being Out of time, take that step forwards again and notice the difference. My advice is to do this a few times before moving on to part two.

Part two: Now ask them to remember an exciting experience from their past. It could be a holiday experience or a party or a birthday. It doesn't matter what the experience is, as long as they have quite strong emotions attached to it. Get them to put that event on their timeline and move the line around so that they are at that point in time. Now get them to close their eyes and remember everything they can about it – what were they feeling, seeing, hearing and saying? Try to put them back there. Once they're there, do the same exercise we did in part one. Step forwards or backwards and notice how different it feels to be In or Out of time. Do this several times until they are comfortable changing their place on the timeline at will.

The reason for doing this is that all experience changes the structure of the brain and brain scans show that, when we strongly imagine something, we are growing synaptic pathways in a very similar way as when we actually experience that same event.

Certainly, having done these exercises myself, I find it noticeably easier to enter into the spirit of the moment as well as to sit back and enjoy watching.

How to motivate an Out of time child

An Out of time child's strength is in planning and responding thoughtfully to anything thrown at them. If they're creative, it's in a thought-through, considered manner. In a crisis they react with clarity and purpose. Not much takes them by surprise and they tend to be well prepared for things. Their strength is also their weakness. They find it hard to be spontaneous and, unless they take steps to counter it, their friends will tend to reflect that fairly serious, slightly removed feel. People are not entirely sure what they're feeling about things because their responses have a measured feel, as though it's been filtered before coming out (which is not a bad description of what's actually going on).

Don't get too frustrated by the fact that your child doesn't relax and enjoy the moment. For them, enjoyment may well come from looking forward to events rather than enjoying the event itself. And as for relaxing, there will be nothing more relaxing for them than to feel like everything's in place and ready.

Don't get too frustrated by the fact that your child doesn't relax and enjoy the moment

How to motivate an In time child

An In time child's strength is their ability to throw themselves into a situation, empathising with those involved. People tend to find them personable and fun, often easy to talk to and a good listener. Their weakness is that they can get so immersed in what's going on that they don't stop to consider the implications and longer-term view. For example, revision may be quite a hard thing to feel motivated about. (It may surprise you to know that some children quite enjoy revising!) The best way to motivate them is to make the consequences as real and as immediate as possible. For example, rather than talking about not getting the results they need at some time in the future, it may be more helpful to talk about how great they will feel straight away by getting some revision done.

Applying the Time perception filter

The situation

Exams are coming up and you want your son or daughter to have a healthy balance between continuing to enjoy life while still getting plenty of revision done.

Out of time (Like Kath)

Often, Out of time children have a good sense of consequence and tend to revise well in advance of an exam because they can see the implications later on if they don't. Parents may get concerned that their child is working too hard and getting too concerned over their exams.

What will help most is regularly reinforcing a healthy overview of the situation – not trivialising the exams but also not over-stating their importance. Sometimes, Out of time children get overly concerned about exams and can become stressed because they can see the bigger picture and may 'catastrophise' (ie see the worst outcomes). It may be helpful in this case to focus on the immediate while keeping a big picture context (eg they will be able to revise better if they get some fresh air) as well as the even bigger picture (eg talk about some people you know who didn't do well in exams but who are still very happy and successful).

In time (Like Atul)

The classic In time child doesn't really feel the implications of future problems and so may well not revise early enough. Nagging rarely seems to produce helpful results. Rather than try to make them see the future implications (something they don't do well) keep it really focused on the immediate issues. Immediate rewards (TV, chocolate, time playing computer games) can be helpful. It may be worth revisiting Chapter 2 and trying Towards or Away from motivations. Talking about the long-term possibilities (eg university, a good job) will have far less impact than talking about what's happening now. In time children may respond well to you getting more involved and being 'in it with them', so find ways of sharing in the revision rather than simply issuing orders and threats.

Summary for using the Time perception filter

Out of time	In time
May seem a bit 'cold' in their immediate responses	Can be strongly influenced by what's happening at the time
Their emotions can be buried, and knowing how they feel about something can be difficult	Their emotions may go up and down and you tend to be aware of how they are feeling
Find ways of making immediate action relevant to long-term outcomes	Find ways of making distant issues (eg exams) relevant to what is happening now
Teach them strategies for 'switching off' and letting go of things that bother them	Teach them strategies for slowing down their responses, eg not reacting quickly to provocation by counting to ten
Praise their focus and perception	Praise their energy
Help them to see the fun of throwing themselves into what's happening	Help them to see their lack of awareness of consequences

Phase 4

Going deeper

VAK: Taking it further

Filters working together

Evolution, not revolution

Chapter 12

VAK: Taking it further

Seeing further, hearing the subleties and going deeper.

Responding in the moment

I said earlier that people are too complicated to fit in a box. It's easy, and very tempting, to say that someone is a 'Visual person' and leave it like that. This statement is always wrong. No matter how visually orientated an individual is, they are always more than that as well. Like all the filters being discussed in this book, the VAK filter is simply a helpful guide. However, because there is an easy-to-spot visual clue as to what's going on inside their head, we can respond immediately to what we see happening.

Once you become aware of the way people's eyes move, you will begin to notice it all the time. You will be able to react in the moment to what you see. If a person who normally looks up looks down when thinking about something, try asking:

"What are you feeling right now about this?"

Or maybe, if you notice that someone who habitually looks to the side looks up when thinking about the question you just posed, you could try asking:

"What is it that you're seeing right now?"

If someone looks to the side, you could ask:

"What are you telling yourself?"

The nice thing about these questions is that they can appear perfectly normal within the conversation and so there's little risk of breaking rapport or looking stupid while trying these out.

Are they lying?

Telling whether someone is lying is a very complicated issue. There are many small signs to watch out for but it takes years of practice to be good at spotting them, and even then it's still very much an art rather than a science. So if someone tells you that they always know when someone lies, it's a pretty safe bet that they are lying! And even here it's not that simple – they might really think they are able to tell, so they are not lying, just deceived.

However, one of the interesting signs to watch out for is to notice the side that people look to when they remember information. For example, one of my children usually looks up (Visual) to remember things. But it's not just 'up', it's usually up and to the left. Her memory space is right there – up and to the left. When she thinks about something and looks up and to the right, she's not accessing memory, she's accessing her imagination. So when she looks up and to the right before saying something I know that at least in part she's probably imagining something rather than remembering it. That doesn't necessarily equate to lying, it may be that she's trying to give the answer that she thinks I want, but it does suggest that the answer isn't a clean representation of what happened.

A little while ago I was working with a school where a very needy child was accused of something. He confessed to it because he thought that was what the slightly scary headteacher wanted and what he thought would make the angry people happy. I noticed that his eye movements didn't follow his normal pattern, suggesting to me that he was trying to say the right thing as opposed to saying what had happened. I stepped in and asked for more details of the actual event and he didn't have them. He hadn't done what he confessed to; he just thought that doing so would make everyone happy.

This process often catches people's imagination and it appears every now and then in the popular press at the same sort of level as an urban myth. A little while ago someone was 'caught' in the TV programme CSI because they 'looked the wrong way' when answering questions. I have two important reservations about this. Firstly, you have to know which way someone normally looks before making any assessment. Don't listen to those who say looking right means one thing and left the other. In my experience, people can be either, in exactly the same way they might be left- or right-handed. So, just like in a film where they are using a lie detector machine, you need to ask a 'calibration question' first to find out which is their normal direction for memory. That means you need to be very confident that they are accessing their memory to answer it. My second reservation goes back to what I've already said: this isn't 'good science' and people are very complicated. So, once more, I encourage you not to take any information you think you gain from this process too seriously!

Patterns of thought processes

If you get to like all of these filters you can take it another step further. Most people have a whole sequence of habitual thought patterns, often shown best when they deal with decisions. For example, one deputy head I worked with answered every question by looking up to the left (Visual memory), then back at me, then off to the right-hand side (Auditory imagination) and then back to me and then answered the question. She did the same pattern every single time I asked her something. What could I deduce from this? I suspected that she felt she had to be very careful what she said in case it was taken the wrong way. I then got slightly pushier and asked if there had been a time when a casual comment had been misinterpreted and caused problems for her in the past. She gasped and said, *"How on earth do you know that?"*.

How did I know that? Her memory was on her left side (she looked up to the left to remember the event I'd just asked about), but before answering she played out how the answer would sound in her head before trusting herself to say it (looking to her right-hand side – Auditory imagination). I'm not saying everyone has such explicit and habitual patterns, but if you start to look out for them you might be surprised by what you see.

What if you learned that your child had a pattern they followed before they made a decision to do something? For example, he might look down, back at you, up to his imagination side, and then glance quickly to the side before responding to a question. His pattern would be to firstly get a feeling for the issue (does it feel right?), then to imagine himself doing it (how does it look?), and then finally to use his auditory imagination to decide what to do. Now you know this, you can work with your child through the entire process.

Imagine you wanted to encourage your child to do some homework before going out. Right at the start, ask questions about how he feels about the issue:

> *"John, what do you feel when you're doing homework? Do you like to get it done, or do you feel bored or frustrated? Do you get a sense of success when it's finished?"*

Then lead him through picturing himself doing it:

> *"Before you decide whether to do it later, just imagine yourself sitting there in 30 minutes time having completed everything. Picture what it will be like to get to that class tomorrow with it all finished."*

Finally, still working with his pattern, ask him auditory questions:

> *"So, tell me, what are you going to do first? Wouldn't you like to be able to tell your friends that it's all finished? Maybe you can be the hero this time and tell them how to do it!"*

Or you can simply go for it all in one question:

> *"So John, are you feeling good about getting on with it right now? I bet you can imagine yourself back at school tomorrow having done this. So what do you want to say to this suggestion?"*

The great thing about this is that, if it works, you've smoothed the road towards your objective. If it doesn't work – if you've misread the signs or your child is simply more complicated than this – then you haven't really lost anything by trying.

Chapter 13
Filters working together

Does one filter suggest another?

Frame of reference and Inside/Outside filters

Whenever I train people to use these filters, there is
a type of question that always arises. I can almost
judge how well a group is handling the new concepts
by when this question is asked. It usually involves
different specifics, but always includes looking for links
between the different filters.

The question may involve gender: *"Do you find
more girls are Outside thinkers?"*. It often tries to link
the Modality (VAK) filter with another filter: *"Are
Kinaesthetic children more likely to be Small chunk?"*.
Sometimes the question makes a link that is fascinating
to explore, though often without any grounding in
reality: *"Towards people must also have an External
frame of reference, mustn't they?"*.

I love these questions because they always reveal the
filters of the questioner. I hate these questions because
I'm never quite sure how to answer them. There are
so many links that seem to make sense on the surface
but there is so little research behind them to be able to
answer clearly. One way to tackle them is to explore
the impact that combinations of filters will have. I
suspect this is the subject for another book because
there is so much that could be investigated. However,

let's explore one such combination together now. What are the implications of the different patterns created when you combine the Inside/Outside filter and the Frame of reference filter?

		Inside/Outside	
		Inside thinker	Outside thinker
Frame of reference	Internal frame of reference	Internal Frame of reference/ Inside thinker	Internal Frame of reference/ Outside thinker
	External frame of reference	External frame of reference/ Inside thinker	External frame of reference/ Outside thinker

There are two ways of benefitting from the exploration of the patterns above. You can think of yourself and notice the impact that your combination has on your parenting or teaching techniques; where you are strong and weak. Or you can think about someone else (eg a child you are having issues with) and recognise the impact that their combination has on their behaviour.

The table below outlines possible benefits and issues associated with each pattern combination:

	Possible benefits	Possible issues
Internal frame of reference and Inside thinker	Able to work alone Good at making decisions and then taking action on them	If they make a poor decision, it may be a while before it comes to light Can feel strongly about an issue but not communicate this to anyone else
Internal frame of reference and Outside thinker	Can make decisions without needing support, but include other people in the process anyway	Sound like they're asking for your opinion when they're actually just processing their own thoughts. This can lead to your frustration that they don't listen after asking for advice

External frame of reference and Inside thinker	Can be good at listening to criticism, taking it on board and then choosing appropriate responses	If they don't handle criticism well, they can dwell on small comments and allow them to fester without others being aware that this is happening
External frame of reference and Outside thinker	Tend to be gregarious, sensitive to other people and eager to talk through any issue to make sure everyone is happy	Can be a bit overwhelming. Always need to talk about everything, never just make a decision and get on with it. Can appear insecure

Can you recognise yourself here?

The benefits and issues shown above are simply a starting point to get you thinking. Can you imagine other possible advantages and disadvantages for each pattern combination?

Chapter 14

Evolution, not revolution

How to introduce any change at any time.

The Relationship filter (Chapter 4) introduced the idea that people can be sorted into the categories Similarities and Differences. There are some important implications that this filter teaches us when it comes to sharing information, especially information about change:

- Around 5-10% of the adult population are strongly similarities based.
- Around 55-65% notice similarities, before then noticing exceptions and seeing some differences.
- Around 20-25% notice differences first and then see similarities.
- Around 5-10% are strongly differences based.

As you study those figures, they tell you that the vast majority of the population are more comfortable with similarities than differences (around 70%). Another 20-25% are still happy with a focus on similarities, even if they don't normally start there. This means that, when we have something new to share, it is much better to start from a place of similarities. We need to start with the known, with the safe, with the familiar and only once that's clearly established begin to introduce the new.

Personally, with a strong Differences pattern (I'm one of the bottom 5-10%), I love it when I'm offered something new.

The very best way to get my attention is to start with a phrase like:

> *"This is something completely new and different from everything you've seen before. It's going to change the way you work and the way you think about work. In fact, nothing is going to be the same ever again!"*

Now you've got my full attention! I would be on the edge of my seat, dribbling slightly, waiting to get started. This is not normal. Most people are at the least uncomfortable with change, many dislike it, some fear it. So to start with the new is not the best way to get their attention.

Let me illustrate this with a story.

Two sets of parents were keen to move house and this involved their children changing schools. Both sets of parents didn't really like the previous school and were excited to be able to make this new start, with new teachers and the opportunity to get away from certain friendships they thought were quite unhelpful to their children.

One set of parents, aware of the sensitivity of moving their child, decided to 'sell' all the positive aspects of the move. They said:

> *"What an amazing opportunity; a chance to meet new friends and make a new start! The journey to school is much shorter so you'll need to walk much less and we're told your new teacher is wonderful, with all sorts of great ideas for how to make learning fun. They even have twice as many computers as your old school!"*

They were quite disappointed with their child's response. Instead of being excited about the new opportunities, he continued to focus on how threatened he was by all the changes, and getting him to school proved to be a nightmare.

The other set of parents decided to focus first on what wasn't changing. They said:

"This school has almost exactly the same number of pupils as your old one. Have you noticed how the uniform is the same except for the colour of the jumper? We'll be able to use the same gym clothes as before. I'm afraid that you're going to continue to struggle with the sunshine in the afternoon because your new class is facing the same way as your old one. We'll still be walking to school every day, though it'll take slightly less time. You'll be glad to know that they have the same sort of computers as your old school and we found out that they use that software you liked."

Although the transition was still uncomfortable, they were pleased with how their child coped with the whole process.

This is a good illustration of saying the same thing with a different focus. The parents in the story may well have a Differences pattern since they were keen to move house. (Similarities pattern people tend to like to stay where they are and simply extend.) However, to help their children, it wasn't what was important to them that was important. It was what was important to the child that was important! Therefore they had to learn to say it in a way that could be well received.

The principle here is: *start with the similarities.* Or, as a colleague helpfully put it recently: *evolution, not revolution.*

From now on, whenever you have something to share, find a way of sharing what is the same first before going on to what is new.

A new project at school

First, you should outline how the new project relates to what has been learned so far. Even if it is completely new material there will be elements that have been dealt with before:

"We're going to move on from this now. [Note: 'moving on from' is much better than tackling something brand new.] Before we do, let's just remind ourselves of what we learned from the last project. Any thoughts? We're going to start thinking about [new topic]. Who can tell me what we already know about this? What else have we already covered that could be relevant?"

"Remember when we started that last project? Remember how some people left it too late? This is the same sort of situation, where you can make it so much easier for yourself by getting involved straight away. Although we're moving on to something new, you're still going to be working in the same way, with small teams supporting each other and, as before, there'll be a mixture of homework and school time. In fact I hope you can see that you're going to be able to use all the experience you've already built up, because the specific skills you learned in the last project are going to be important to your success in this new one."

A new teacher or a parent's new partner

As we saw in the story, it is common for adults to want to impress a child with all the good things about a change. However, to do this usually involves emphasising the very things that could cause stress – all the changes. Start off with similarities rather than differences and emphasise all the things that aren't going to change first:

> "Because I know just what you like, I think you're going to like Mr Smith. He's got just the same sense of fun/care/interests/hairstyle [anything you can think of that's the same as the previous person] as Mrs Jones. Isn't it good that they haven't had to change any of your timetable? Hasn't he got the same colour eyes/shoes/hair/car as Mrs Jones? I noticed that he seems to like the same sort of things as you and has a very similar sense of humour."

Sometimes all it takes is a few carefully considered words related to what is the same to win over otherwise cautious children. Evolution, not revolution is a great rule of thumb.

However, as you talk, if you notice that your child is switched off and not engaged with you then it might be worth trying to emphasise the differences and see if that works better.

Chapter 15

A filter interview

How to take someone through all the filters in one go.

Sometimes it is helpful to quickly get a measure of someone's filter patterns in one go. This can be done in less than ten minutes by conducting an interview. These interviews are usually great fun and informative when conducted in the right way and in a good environment. There are a few things to be careful of:

- If you aren't the parent, it is important to keep everyone informed. Some schools I've worked with have invited parents in to be involved as I've chatted with the child. If you are a teacher, at the very least talk to the headteacher about what you're doing and make sure you have their support.

- The concept of a 'profile' is often not helpful since people tend to use it to refer to nature rather than behaviour. These filters are about behaviour rather than character. As such there is plenty of room for people to change. (We don't belong in boxes, no matter how cleverly the boxes have been created.)

- To make this useful, the bland results need translating into something practical – a list of what to do and say differently for that child.

- As explained in Chapter 2, sometimes the interviewee gives unexpected answers and the temptation is to spend time digging deeper and deeper trying to find an answer that makes sense. Usually all this does is keep the conversation going until the questioner hears the filter pattern they are looking for. My research has repeatedly shown that, the longer someone takes to ascertain the filter pattern, the more likely they are to decide that the person matches their own pattern. It's better to leave that question and go on to something you do understand. (The metaphor I used in Chapter 1 is helpful here. It's a bit like a meal where you come across a bone. You could spend a long time chewing on the bone trying to digest it when actually there's the rest of the meal waiting to be eaten. It's better to move on and leave the bone on the side of the plate for now. You can always come back to it later if you haven't been filled by the rest of the meal!) As a rule of thumb, if you take longer than ten minutes to conduct the interview you're getting too bogged down.

- Look out for the strong filter patterns, the obvious ones. Understanding these will make the biggest difference. Where someone is more balanced, it makes less difference to become aware of or to seek to explore a different side of that filter.

- Share the insights the interview has given at the end rather than after each question.

- I am always very open about what's going on and discuss the results with the interviewee. Sometimes I work with young children and I will still chat through the things I notice – they often still surprise me with their insight into who they are and what they're good at. I don't like the idea of this being secret information.

Having voiced those concerns, the actual interview is very simple to conduct. All you have to do is pay close attention to what they say, being careful not to filter it in any way (otherwise you'll simply be holding up a mirror and seeing yourself rather than them). The following questions are a simplified form of the questions in each chapter.

It may be worth referring to the relevant chapter if you are not clear about the wording below.

One last word of advice: have a pen and paper with you. Most people can't hold all the information in their heads, even if they think they will when they begin. It's worth telling the child that you're going to take notes so that you can give good feedback at the end. Once completed, I nearly always give the parent or teacher the notes so that they have a record of it all. As well as being helpful, it also makes it very clear that I haven't kept a written record of what was learned.

Direction filter

"What do you look for in a friend?" (Or you can ask about a school or a lesson, etc.)

Get three answers.

"Why is [what they said] important to you?"

Insert the very word(s) they used into the question, being careful not to change them at all. Do this for all three answers you got from the first question.

Listen for whether they talk about what they *want* or what they *don't want*.

Frame of reference filter

"How do you know when you've done something well?"

Listen for whether they talk about what they *just know internally* or what they get *from others* or a mixture of the two. If a mixture, notice which they say first since that will be more important for them.

If Internal, they often point towards themselves. If External, they often make open-handed gestures including others.

A nice follow-up question is:

"Where do you feel that?"

Internal frame patterns will point to somewhere on their body (heart, head, stomach). External frame patterns simply don't understand the question.

Relationship filter

"Compare this class to last year's class."

Similarities children will talk about what's stayed *the same*. Differences children will talk about what's *changed*.

Or:

Choose two objects that are quite similar but have some differences (for example, I often choose two similar ballpoint pens) and say to the child:

"Tell me about these two objects."

Do they talk about the similarities or differences? If both, which do they notice first?

VAK (Modality) filter

"Tell me about last Christmas. [Or your last holiday, or birthday.]"

Watch their eyes. Do they look up, sideways or down to remember? If they simply look straight at you and answer then make the question harder, eg:

"Tell me about last Boxing Day." or "Tell me about the day after Boxing Day."

Avoid questions that may automatically focus them on the visual, auditory or kinaesthetic experience. For example, *"Tell me about your football match yesterday"* is a poor question since it may focus on the kinaesthetic memory.

Also look at the way they are sitting, the pace with which they answer, the tone of their voice and how they look (clothes, shoes, hair brushed, etc).

Inside/Outside filter

"When you have to choose something (like the topic for a project, or what to wear to a party), do you tend to talk about the options with someone else first or do you tend to make your own decisions?"

What they want to do first is the main clue. If they aren't clear or aren't sure then talk about a specific example, eg:

"What did you want for your last birthday? Did you choose that because someone else had one? Or was it simply something that you wanted?"

Chunk size filter

"If you were to start something new (eg a new topic at school), would you want to know the details or the overview first?"

"Tell me about your last holiday."

Now listen closely to whether they talk about the destination and *general* accommodation, etc or focus very quickly on small *details*.

Sometimes it's hard for people to know how to answer this and so you can help by holding out your hands and explaining that, in one hand, you're holding the name of the place you're planning to go to for a holiday and, in the other, the list of what they will do on the first day – which would they most like to see first? Watch the eyes on this one. Their gaze to one hand or the other may tell you more about what they want than their verbal answer does.

Options/Procedures filter

"Why did you choose to watch that on TV?"

"Why do you like wearing those clothes?"

"Why do you like [a friend]?"

Options pattern children will answer by giving a set of *criteria*. Procedures pattern children will answer by telling you the *story* of how they made that choice.

NB Some can do both in one answer and so belong somewhere in the middle of the spectrum.

Time perception filter

"Imagine you could point to your past. Which direction would you point in?"

"Now imagine you could point to your future. Which direction would you point in?"

You may need to ask the child to 'move' the lines so that they can see them both. (See Chapter 11 for more information.)

"Draw a line from your past into your future."

It may help them to do so with their finger rather than just in their imagination.

"Does that line go through you, or in front of you?"

In time children draw the line going through a part of their body. Out of time children draw it in front of them.

Chapter 16

What next?

Well done! You may be surprised to learn how many people don't ever finish a book.

Now you have the tools and the knowledge to do three things:

Play to their strengths

You now know more clearly what the children in your life are good at. Make the most of their strengths by focusing on what they can do well. Whatever you do, don't make the mistake of recognising what they are good at only to leave that aside and focus on their weaknesses. Schools across the country are doing that. They are taking children out of music lessons or drama lessons or PE lessons and using the time to work harder on what they are failing at – usually maths or English. This is an appalling mistake! I have a friend whose daughter is currently missing music lessons because she performs poorly in English. They justify it because she's good at music and so doesn't need to be there. However, she's also seeing the Educational Psychologist because she's 'depressed'. No wonder, if she's spending all her time reinforcing the fact that she is bad at things!

> *All the young animals attended school. They were so excited to be there and loved competing at the different tasks, showing their friends what they were good at. However,*

the squirrel was brilliant at climbing and so they gave him extra swimming lessons where he was extremely weak. The mole was wonderful at digging and so they took him out of digging lessons since he obviously didn't need them and gave him extra flying classes. The trout was so useless at climbing that they took her out of everything else and focused just on that, including keeping her behind after school every day to give her more time to improve.

Concern arose from the parents that their children were unhappy and beginning to be difficult at home. Knowing that bad behaviour often comes from a poor self-image, the school worked even harder to help them achieve at least some level of success in those areas where they were failing so badly.

Be a better parent or teacher

Learn how to tap into your children's patterns. You'll probably never be good at their pattern but you can involve them so much more by learning to include their styles of thinking. The only way I know to do this effectively is to practice. Trying to say things in different ways in the car as you drive is a good way of practising (any observers will just think you're on the phone).

Remember, none of these patterns is intrinsically better than or worse than any other. They are simply more appropriate or helpful in different contexts. Remember too that you will automatically favour your own set of patterns over different ones. You almost can't help doing so. Therefore try to deliberately value those who have different filter patterns from you. You need them – you need their insights, their strengths and their perspectives (even though you secretly feel they're a bit flaky!).

Share what you learn with the children

Help the children to understand themselves better and to work with their strengths and understand their weaknesses. I often see great results from helping children to understand exactly why they behave in the ways that they do. Trust them with the knowledge rather than seeing it as a possible way of manipulating them to 'do the right thing'. (What 'the right thing' is, of course, depends on your patterns.)

My final piece of advice? Use the filters! What a shame to invest both the cost and the time in reading this book and then move on to the next thing without putting the learning into practice. Start simply with one filter, look out for examples of it happening, and practise working in harmony with the filter you observe. Only move on to another filter when you are feeling confident about observing and using the first one. It will also make a huge difference for you if you discover your own filter patterns and begin to learn to respond more flexibly.

Who knows, maybe the relationship with the child you're struggling with could be transformed by just observing one strong filter at work. Remember Edward? It only took one filter to make the difference.

Also by Justin Collinge

Knowing you, Knowing them
Understanding and motivating at work

Justin applies the same understanding and knowledge you have just enjoyed from *Understanding Edward* to a work context. This book is full of practical and insightful advice to help you manage or lead your team.

Praise for *Knowing you, Knowing them*:

"If you want a straightforward, no-nonsense explanation of why people are motivated in different ways then this is the book for you. At its core are NLP [neuro-linguistic programming] principles, but Justin has written this without any over-the-top NLP speak or jargon. The structure enables you to dip in and dip out. The examples are uncomplicated and clear."

Kimberley Hare, author of *The Trainer's Toolkit*

"The tone the author uses is so friendly, down-to-earth, practical and warm it feels like a conversation over a cup of tea – I really enjoyed it and am valuing the effects I am now creating in my own day-to-day business with people. Highly recommended! Try it now!"

Heider Imam, author of *47 Moments of Inspiration*

Coming soon: *Discover your filters*

An online system for discovering your filter patterns and receiving help to know exactly where those patterns will support or hinder you, and what to do about it.

If you want to know when this becomes available and get a free login to discover one of your key filter patterns, email us and we'll send you details as soon as it is available.

Email: filters@ProvenICT.com

Bibliography

McTaggart, Lynne, *The Intention Experiment*, Harper Element, 2007

Migliore, Michele, Novara, Gaspare and Tegolo, Domenico, 'Single neuron binding properties and the magical number 7' in *Hippocampus*, Volume 18 Issue 11, Pages 1122-1130, Published online 4 August 2008

Rock, David, *Your Brain at Work: Strategies for Overcoming Distraction, Regaining Focus, and Working Smarter All Day Long*, Harper Business, 2009

Stavrinou, Maria et al, *Evaluation of Cortical Connectivity During Real and Imagined Rhythmic Finger Tapping*, Patras University, 2007

Wyman, Pat, *Learning vs Testing: Strategies That Bridge the Gap*, Zephyr Press, 2001

Woodsmall, Wyatt, *Metaprograms*, Next Step Press, 1998

Woodsmall, Wyatt, *The Science of Advanced Behavioral Modelling*, Next Step Press, 1998

5940202R00088

Printed in Great Britain
by Amazon.co.uk, Ltd.,
Marston Gate.